INFERNALIA

Infernalia

The Collected Writings of

MICHAEL ROSE

Introduction by

PETER H. GILMORE

THIRD EDITION

UNDERWORLD AMUSEMENTS

isbn: 978-0-9885536-9-9

Cover illustration and
"Accoutrement of the Mass of Saint Francis"
illustration by Daniel Byrd © 2015.
www.CoffinRust.com

Title & author name lettering by Paul Slagle, 2015.
www.PaulSlagle.com

Introduction by Peter H. Gilmore © 2008.
www.ChurchOfSatan.com

Cover and interior designed by Kevin I. Slaughter.

Most of the materials contained herein originally appeared in the magazines From The Pit, The Black Flame, The Cloven Hoof, *and* The Black Pun-Kin. *Most appear in more or less the same form in which they originally appeared, others have been revised.*

Published by Underworld Amusements *of Baltimore.*
www.UnderworldAmusements.com

DEDICATION

To three wise men who have taught me so much...

Anton Szandor LaVey
H.L. Mencken
Friedrich Nietzsche

To dear friends who have in so many ways influenced the essays written here...

Peter H. Gilmore
Peggy Nadramia
Blanche Barton
Robert Lang
Diana DeMagis

To the many members of the Church of Satan hierarchy who have meant so much to me over the years.

And last, but most certainly not least...

To my wife who took up the task of retyping and editing this collection at a time when I was ready to abandon the project as a bloody nuisance.

CONTENTS

9 • Introduction
13 • Invocation
15 • Bigotry
17 • A Real Death Cult
19 • Hunters & Ecology
21 • A Quest for Democracy?
23 • Choose Your Devils Wisely
26 • A Little Satanic Cinema
28 • Satanism & Racism
30 • Taking the Christ Out of Christmas
32 • The Lion & The Child
34 • Law & Order
36 • Democracy
38 • Who Said What?
40 • A Pack of Lies, and a Declaration of War
42 • Persecution
45 • An Answer to Urban Blight
46 • Kill a Cow for Satan?
48 • Give Me That Old Time Religion
50 • The Church of the Passed Buck
53 • Politics
55 • The Debt of the West?
56 • A Poisonous "Treat"
58 • Shall We Give Thanks?
59 • A Fallacious Foundation
62 • Education
64 • Redeeming the Count
67 • Heretics & Madmen: The Writings of Thomas Szasz
69 • Same Old Song & Dance
70 • Objections to Objectivism
73 • Manfred vs Faust
75 • Traditional Satanism?
77 • Heaven & Hell

79 • Thoughts on Free Will
81 • Sacred?
84 • Nihilism
86 • Paganism & The Deification of Culture
89 • Entering the Abyss: The Psychology of Magic
93 • Smells Like a Dead Junkie
94 • Legitimizing Lovecraft
96 • Robert E. Howard: Satanic Skald
99 • The Enemy
101 • Killing Time
104 • Satanic Victims?
106 • Satanic Brotherhood?
108 • Confessions of a LaVey Lackey
110 • Ritual to Secure Cooperation
112 • Lies I Learned in School
115 • Bitter Fruit
118 • Maybe It's Not So Bitter After All
121 • Art?
123 • How to be a Satanic Breeder
125 • Don't Drug That Monkey
128 • 'Tis The Season to Be Stupid
129 • On the Uses of Fascism
132 • To Be, Or Not To Be...Evil
133 • The Christians are Coming! Or are They?
136 • A Better Place
146 • Of Gods and Gods
148 • Film Noir, Tragedy and The Satanist
150 • The Satanist in the Garden
152 • Dueling Dualities
158 • It's Not a Badge of Honor
160 • W.W.A.D.
163 • The Mass of Saint Francis
172 • Credo for the Modern Man

INTRODUCTION

Magister Michael Rose is not a shy fellow. If he's in a room, it is simple to spot him — look for the massive man towering over all present, his face touched with a knowing smile. He was raised in America's "Bible Belt" but was not compelled to conform or in any way "become one" with the environment surrounding him as he matured. This Rose saw the fertilizer of Christian doctrine around him and recognized it for the shit that it is, instinctively knowing that it was emphatically not a healthy regimen for his own growth. How did he manage in this intellectual and aesthetic desert? He didn't need the support of any fellowship; instead, he discovered that there were like minds by reading books—that's where his peers were.

He haunted the local bookstores, befriending the owners who would then put aside used books that they knew would pique his interest. His Lesser Magic worked, and so his library grew and provided him with an ever broadening perspective from which to cast his cynical glance upon the cretins he regularly encountered. He also discovered the musical works of the great Western composers, and found inspiration from the likes of Wagner, Beethoven, Bruckner and the other giants of orchestral writing. No, there was no whining for a community, no begging for understanding, no morose introversion. Instead, he held most of the locals in deserved contempt and made his own way, being an exemplar of the Satanist who creates his own horizons.

During the years of the "Satanic Panic" Magister Rose published his own small magazine entitled "From The Pit." It was issued from 1992-1996 CE, and presented pithy essays that provided Satanists with a healthy draught of well-targeted misanthropy and third-side stances. Subsequently, collections were issued, but now for the first time you have them in one potent volume. In his writing, Rose philosophizes with a pitchfork, skewering a panoply of sacred cows and roasting their empty ideological carcasses over Hell fires until they are done to the proper degree. No coddling of slow thinkers; no elaborate attempts at persuasion, just broadsides aimed at whatever roused his ire that came into his purview.

The volume you have at hand of ideas forged when Satanism was given far less credence will demonstrate the bravery of Magister Rose, and I'm certain that you will enjoy the body slams he delivers to a broad range of offenders against his sense of justice and aesthetics. Enjoy your time reading from our Conan of Satanic concepts. You'll find that amidst the excoriations there are flashes of sardonic humor and even touches of poetic vision, much as those indulged in by a wise conqueror who views the sun setting on the battlefield wherein his latest victory has been won. You are invited to share in his triumph.

Magus Peter H. Gilmore
July 4, XLIII AS

INFERNALIA

INVOCATION

Oh mighty Satan, Lord of the world,
We call to thee.
Arise and come forth!
Marshall thy hosts,
And send forth the Infernal Legions
For the apocalypse is upon us!
The righteous have had their era.
Now is come the Age of Satan!
Oh, Black Angel of the Bottomless Pit
The time has come for you to rise
And bring devastation in thy wake.
The worshipers of the dead god
Those deniers of the flesh
Those despisers of life
Poison tongued slanderers of pleasure
Have infested the world.
They await thy coming, oh Abaddon
Foolishly believing that it heralds their victory.
A victory that shall never come!
We call ye forth to break their rule
And end the madness of their age.
Be unto us a beacon in this wilderness of fear and ignorance.
We beckon thee Oh great beast from the outer dark.
Come, with thy brothers, and thy children.
Restore justice to a world of laws
Vengeance to a world of mercy
And purity to a world of corruption.

BIGOTRY

The time has come to assert who, and what, we are. We must no longer allow our enemies to define us as they see fit.

I can't remember how many times I have been asked such inanities as, "Do you really worship the Devil?" or "You people don't really sacrifice animals to Satan, do you?" If I were to ask one of these tiresome dolts whether they really ate Jesus during the communion ritual they would probably think me an idiot, and be quite offended as well, yet they expect us to put up with *their* perpetual idiocies without complaint.

It is likely that if you were to approach someone on the street and ask them about Satanism they would probably tell you that Satanists kill and eat children during orgiastic blood rituals. Sadly, most people cannot see that such accusations are nothing new. In Nero's Rome Christians were themselves subject to the same kind of stories. In medieval Europe Jews, gypsies and eccentrics were burned at the stake because of such hysteria. In the United States, Mormons were lynched by angry mobs that believed such rumors.

Throughout human history such stories abound. The fact that the majority of child abusers and murderers in America have either considered themselves to be Christian, or were actually members of some Christian church, appears to be lost on the gullible herds who readily believe every lurid yarn about Satanism; no matter how far-fetched it is. People who wouldn't dream of accusing a Jew of ritual infanticide think nothing of laying such charges on our doorstep. Men and women who loudly sing the praises of religious freedom will heartily endorse attempts to outlaw Satanism. What it all boils down to is this: according to the Christian worldview you have the right to be any kind of Christian you choose. Any desire to follow a different path is evidence of your total depravity.

Why does such bigotry exist? Because they fear us, that's why! We are not like them. We are individuals, and as such are harder to control. We don't conform to their accepted patterns of thought, not even to the accepted modes of "non-conformity". We refuse to yield to the social indoctrination, which is foisted upon us through education, television and pop-culture. We are the ultimate horror to a world of sheep for we have, of our own volition, forsaken the herd to live as we choose. It isn't only the Christians who despise us. Neo-Pagans, Wiccans and assorted other New-Agers have jumped on the Satanist bashing bandwagon. These groups claim that we are merely knee-jerk Antichrists existing in some symbiotic relationship with the Christians. This is ridiculous. Satanism is a religion of iconoclasm rather than idolatry. We worship no God, or Goddess outside of ourselves, and we topple idols of more conventional religions. The only reason we pay little attention to them is that their influence on this culture is insignificant and thus we have bigger fish to fry, as it were. We are indeed Antichrists, for we stand against Christian values, but we do not merely gainsay any Christian ideas that we hear. We have a comprehensive, and well-developed philosophy by which we live. This philosophy is set forth in *The Satanic Bible* for all to see, although the Christian majority would seek to deny people access to this book by bullying stores into not selling it. This of course makes it much easier to lie about us.

It isn't always easy being a Satanist, but bear in mind what Nietzsche said—*"That which does not kill me makes me stronger".* As you grow in that strength you will come to understand many things. In time you will come to an understanding of the God that you are. If you persevere I think you will find that it was well worth all the trouble and aggravation brought on by contact with lesser men and women. Rejoice in their hatred for it is a badge of honor.

A REAL DEATH CULT

Few people hate the summer as much as I do, but there is one thing about the end of the summer that never fails to fill me with loathing. That thing is the Jerry Lewis Telethon. Now I don't actually watch this horror show, nor am I one of those who bemoan the fact that it preempts the shows that they usually watch. No, the Jerry Lewis Telethon is like Christmas, it is all around you. Posters depicting sick children, and shameless pleas for pity are all around us for a time. What bothers me most about this great cultural event is that it illustrates the pervasive influence of what Nietzsche called Chandala moralities upon our present culture.

A man stands before the public and pleads with them to help prolong the lives of sick children, and the public responds by sending in millions of dollars. Nobody asks to what end we are preserving their lives. Nor do they ask what is to be gained by saving their lives. No, that would be considered cruel and heartless. Has it never occurred to these people that if all those with genetically transmitted diseases were allowed to die without issue that there would be substantially fewer cases of those diseases in the next generation? By prolonging their lives do you not merely prolong the suffering? Would the world be diminished by the deaths of these children? If we answer honestly we must say no. Heartless and cruel though such sentiment may be we must admit that it would be enriched by such deaths. When the weak and sick die the genetic health of the species cannot help but be improved. Conversely, every such worthless life that is prolonged weakens the species and pollutes the bloodlines of generations yet to come. Some might read this and leap to the conclusion that I am in favor of euthanizing such children, yet this is not the case. I do not care about them. If their families wish to provide the means by which their lives might be prolonged, that is entirely up to them. Compulsory sterilization of the irreparably defective would satisfy me. If the attitudes at the root of the desire to prolong such lives could be changed then nature would be allowed to take its course and eliminate such individuals from the gene pool.

Earlier I called the show a "great cultural event". By this I mean it is like a sort of religious festival. This show parades these miserable wretches as living icons of the wretchedness and suffering, which are venerated by the Chandala hordes. Another example of this Chandala foolishness is the recurring spectacles associated with outbreaks of famine. These situations are simple enough. Wherever you have famine you have too many people living in an area that cannot sustain such a number. Nature has a time-tested method of resolving such problems—the strongest and the smartest get the available food, the rest must die! Man doesn't think that such a principle is fair, as if nature is concerned with such notions as fairness, so he interferes in the natural order and only manages to make everything suffer. They will talk endlessly of the need to find a solution to the world's problems when the solution is right before their eyes—let nature take its course.

Man, under the anti-nature influence of the Chandala systems, has tipped the balance of nature to a dangerous degree. Nature will one day restore the balance, and when it does billions will die. This is good, for the world is seriously overpopulated. After the storm passes only the smartest and strongest will remain to rebuild the human race. Our salvation lies not in the death of a mad Jew some two millennia ago, but in the rejection of Chandala values; in an acceptance of nature as it is. Be alert to the anti-natural biases of the modern world. Learn to be harsh when necessary, for nature itself is a harsh overlord. Trust in your instincts. Reason is a tool, not an end in itself. Keep these things in mind and maybe when the storm comes you will be found worthy to survive. No one can stand against nature. You can stand with it, or you can fall!

HUNTERS & ECOLOGY

One of the sillier things that I keep hearing is that deer hunters are simply performing the vital role that was once performed by wolves and other such predators, and in so doing improve the genetic health of the species. To hear these hunters talk you would think that they do the wolf's job even better than the wolves did. In fact, nothing could be further from the truth.

Modern man no longer hunts for survival. Even if he eats the meat of his kills, many modern hunters are primarily interested in the *sport* of it. The fact of the matter is that human hunters are not at all like wolves or cougars. The instinct of such predators is pure. The instincts of these humans are all too often perverted to such a degree that they bear scant resemblance to the sound instincts of natural predators.

Let's take a look at the differing results of human hunting and natural predation. When wolves, or other predators, hunt they have but one goal: to eat. They will kill and eat the first animal that they can drag down. As a consequence of this the bulk of the animals killed through natural predation are the very young, the very old, or the sick. The human hunter argues that he does not kill does or fawns, and that this is somehow supposed to be beneficial. His reasons for this have much more to do with the fact that a well antlered buck makes a more impressive trophy, but more on this later. If you look at things superficially the killing of young animals might seem to be antithetical to the survival of the species but in reality it is not. Among most animals more young are born than can reasonably be expected to live. To keep most of these young animals alive disrupts the balance of nature.

The human hunter goes out in the woods with his high-powered rifles, sex scent lures and other goodies with only one objective: to kill the biggest and strongest buck that he can find. The human hunter will allow countless weaker animals to pass by unmolested in his single-minded quest to bag a trophy buck. It is this which shows that the human hunter's self proclaimed goal of improving the health of deer herds is a lie because in doing this he is removing the best genes from the breeding pool. In the final analysis it becomes obvious that man's hunting habits are contrary to normal, natural predation.

I do not have a problem with those humans who hunt on a subsistence basis. If a man is hunting for the purpose of eating rather than bragging he will wind up doing as the wolves do because it is easier to kill old, sick or crippled animals. It is an unfortunate reality that many men are so alienated from the true predatory impulse that only a twisted and perverted shadow of it remains. In the final analysis, man's hunting is anti-nature; a wolf's is not.

A QUEST FOR DEMOCRACY?

As the western world watches the fragmentation of the old Soviet Union, it seems to me that everybody and his brother seems at risk of dislocating their shoulders while patting themselves on the back. There is an orgy of self-congratulation going on as the various interest groups claim to be the direct cause of the demise of communism.

The Christians claim that communism's collapse was caused by the desire of the masses to worship Jesus. Never mind the fact that most of these people are not Christians. The political advocates of democracy claim that the people's desire for democratic government is responsible. One would think that after seventy-four years of inept bureaucratic government just about anything would seem an improvement. Big business claims that a desire for capitalism brought it all about. Again, things were so bad that I think the general attitude was "no change can be for the worse".

Instead, I attribute the fall of the Soviet Union to two factors. One is the aforementioned incompetence of the Soviet bureaucracy. A less inept government might have been able to linger a bit longer. Their inability to feed and amuse the masses created unrest, thus opening the way for ever-increasing decay. The second factor is nationalism. The Marxist theory doesn't take into account the tribalism inherent in the human animal. One manifestation of this tribalism, but certainly not the only one, is nationalism. The Soviet Union attempted to fuse several nations into a single nation. Such an effort can succeed only so long as the masses can be distracted with "bread & circuses", or held together by an iron-fisted ruler. The Soviet Union couldn't do this and thus allowed nationalism to rear its head.

All over the world, societies are fragmenting along national/ethnic lines. Nations that were formed by dividing, or joining these ethnic/national groups are restructuring themselves according to this ancient tribal imperative. Many people say that it cannot happen here in the United States, but it already is. Just open your eyes. The rise of the "hyphenated American" is one aspect of it. The reluctance of various groups to give up native languages & customs is another. This is a nation of refugees. Abstract allegiance to the American ideal is dissipating rapidly.

Do not make the mistake of thinking that nationalism is the inevitable end. It isn't. It is just one step. After nationalism asserts itself, ever-smaller divisions will arise. These smaller divisions are ethnic, religious, linguistic, political etc. People will always seek out those like them. At first, nationalism gives people something in common. Soon they will realize that just because they are from the same nation as their fellow citizens they don't have much in common. The man that seemed your "brother" yesterday will be your mortal enemy tomorrow.

I welcome the new tribalism. It signals a return to a more natural order of things.

CHOOSE YOUR DEVILS WISELY

Often, once we get people to understand that Satanists don't worship the devil, or even believe in the devil, but rather, have an affinity for the ideas that Satan represents; there is still an immense gap for these outsiders to cross before they truly understand. This great chasm between them and us is reflected in comments like "How can you admire the Devil?" The problem is one of perception. Most people simply do not perceive the Satanic as we do. The average person, raised within a more or less Christian context, sees Satan as the image of all that is wrong with the world. However, the image and idea of Satan has come to us in various forms from antiquity. The simple Christian concept of the fallen angel eager to destroy everything good is not the only one. Whole volumes can be, and have been, written about the evolution of the idea of Satan in the West. What follows is but a brief overview.

The ancient Hebrews saw Satan as the enemy of man, not god. To them, Satan was a sort of prosecuting attorney pleading the case against man; he was just another angel. However, with the fall of Babylon, when the captive Jews were exposed to the Persian cult of Zoroastrianism, the Jewish conception of Satan was forever changed.

The Zoroastrians held that there were two opposing forces in the world. Ahura-Mazda, or Ormuzd, represented light and goodness. Angra-Mainyu, or Ahriman, represented darkness and evil. After coming into contact with this dualistic religion the Jews forever saw Satan as the enemy of god and man; an anti-god. The image of Satan became forever enmeshed with that of Ahriman. It was in this dualized Judaism that Christianity arose. Even after Christianity had evolved beyond being a mere heretical sub sect of Judaism they kept the image of Satan as an anti-god.

These early Christians saw Satan as a slavering monster seeking to lead them into temptation and sin, and in so doing to separate them from god. It would be a mistake to think that the image of Satan has remained unchanged since the advent of Christianity. The Christian concept of Satan has been modified by contact with various Pagan religions. According to the rather limited world-view of this rabble, the gods worshiped by non-Christians must be devils. As a consequence, Satan took on various attributes of these deities. One of the most prominent contributors to the "new & improved" Satan was Pan. As you might imagine, the early Christians were shocked and horrified by the sensuality and, at least by their standards, sexual immorality of the Greeks. It is only natural that the bestial aspects of the Greek nature & fertility god would come to characterize Satan in Christian minds. To get an idea of the severity of the sexual codes amongst the early Christians read Augustine's *The City of God*, if you can stomach it.

Besides a virulent hatred of sex, and other fleshly pleasures, these wretched little bigots also hated all learning and philosophy. They had their holy books so no others were needed. Other books merely spread the lies of the Devil, or encouraged men to sins, such as pride. As a result, Europe was plunged into a long age of ignorance; and Satan became associated with secular wisdom. Thus, in the Christian world, Satan becomes the bestower of pleasures, and the dispenser of worldly knowledge.

Another role Satan found himself cast in during the middle ages was that of the clown. This view was most common among the lower castes. The form of these tales is fairly simple: Satan tries to trick someone into surrendering his or her soul. Somehow this simple rustic manages to turn the tables on Old Nick and send him back to Hell with egg on his face. Not too long ago a country music song presented an updated version of this story, so you can see that this view is still alive. As I mentioned, this view was most common amidst the peasantry. It gave them a sense of power, something that they were denied in life. If they were smarter than the devil, surely they were smarter than the lord of the manor. The same attitude is still quite prominent in the makeup of the lowest of the low. While the rabble tried to make of Satan the butt of jokes, the official status of Satan remained unchanged.

As the middle ages gave way to the Renaissance a more familiar conception of Satan begins to emerge. As the dark fog of ignorance was dispelled by the ever-increasing iconoclasm of the elite, Satan became an increasingly human figure. No more the slavering monster, Satan had become the majestic and aristocratic Lord Satan that so many of us hold near and dear. During this period this heroic Satan makes his appearance in John Milton's immortal masterwork, *Paradise Lost*. Who can forget Satan's defiant proclamation "To reign is worth ambition though in Hell: Better to reign in Hell, than serve in Heav'n." While many argue that Milton did not intend to glorify Satan, there can be no doubt that Milton's Satan is one of literature's great heroes.

Our conception of Satan came to its fullest flowering in the works of the Romantics, particularly the so-called *"Satanic School"*, which was personified by the poet George Gordon, more commonly known as Lord Byron. The Satan of Byron, and the other Romantics, is most certainly not the Satan of the Christians. The pathetically narrow-minded Christians simply do not understand our Satan, the Satan of the Romantics. That is why they cannot understand our sense of the Satanic. They are too backwards, scarcely past the medieval perception of Satan, if that far along. We have gone beyond them. We no longer speak the same language. Our Satan contains elements of theirs, but he is also so much more. Do not debase yourself with their Devil. There is a better alternative. Choose your Devils wisely.

A LITTLE SATANIC CINEMA

If you are looking for a good movie featuring Satanism you should look for *The Seventh Victim*. They didn't get it 100% right, and one of the maddening things is that "evil" is not allowed to win, but aside from that, it was a more accurate than normal portrayal of Satanists. One of the things that really set this movie apart though, is that in the end the Satanists win.

The story is about a teenage girl who leaves her boarding school to search for her missing sister in New York. During the course of her search she meets an odd assortment of people—her brother-in-law, a poet, and a psychiatrist who runs an expensive clinic. They discover that the Sister joined a group of Satanists. The Satanists meanwhile are trying to convince the sister to commit suicide for betraying them.

Towards the end of the movie there is a scene that is particularly memorable to me. It appears to me to be a scene designed to get the movie past the review board. It has no real bearing on the rest of the movie, and cannot be taken seriously except by the most arrogant of Christians. I have transcribed the scene for you below. Unless stated otherwise the poet comes across as smarmily self-righteous, the doctor is humble, and the Satanist is reasonable and civil. The scene arrives as the two men, who are searching for the missing sister, are about to leave the home of one of the Satanists, having interrupted a gathering.

POET: The Devil worshipers, the lovers of evil. It's a joke, a pathetic little joke.

SATANIST: We haven't asked your opinion.

POET: Well I propose to give it to you anyway. You're a poor, wretched group of people who have taken a wrong turning.

SATANIST: Wrong? Who knows what is wrong or right? If I prefer to believe in Satanic majesty and power who can deny me? What proof can you bring that good is superior to evil?

POET: (hesitates) It's hard to put into words, but you're wrong.

SATANIST: One proof.

DOCTOR: I'll prove you wrong. This afternoon Jason (the poet) and I were talking together and I remembered certain phrases from childhood. Simple, half forgotten words. It was the Lord's Prayer. I'm a physician, yet not I, nor any of my colleagues, no matter how learned, ever found a substitute for those few words as a rule for human relationships. You might remember them.

POET: (reverently) Forgive us our trespasses, as we forgive those who trespass against us.

(At this point the Satanist is shown looking rather nervous and upset.)

DOCTOR: There's a sentence for you people from that same prayer. Lead us not into temptation, but deliver us from evil.

(Now the Satanists are shown cringing away from these words, filled with guilt and shame.)

Thus are the Satanists *defeated* by the *word of God.*

What's so Satanic about that you ask. Well, I'll tell you. That isn't quite the end of the movie. After that scene, the woman kills herself while, in the next room, her husband and sister, oblivious to her fate, declare their love for one another. In my book that makes the Satanists winners. Their goal, the woman's suicide, is accomplished.

Now, let's go back to that other scene for a moment. As I said earlier, nobody can take it seriously. Does hearing the Lord's Prayer fill you with guilt & shame? Of course not, the very idea is ridiculous. Now ask yourself, who is the most reasonable character? One might expect it to be the doctor, a man of science, but is it? No. The doctor merely offers up a prayer to prove his point. The poet? Again, no, he just says, "you're wrong" and lets it go at that. No, the most rational by far is the Satanist. After being interrupted in his lair he coolly questions his accusers. He meets their self-righteous assertions with the one question they cannot answer—where is your proof?

The reactions of the Satanists to the prayer were a sop to the review board. The actions of the Satanist are an admirable model for our own reactions when confronted with ignorance.

SATANISM & RACISM

I received a newsletter from an allegedly "Satanic" organization based in Florida. This newsletter was long on news about the KKK, and Nazism but almost devoid of anything else. This same group also believes that the "Aryan" race is descended from angels, and is therefore destined to rule the world. This is not true Satanism. There is nothing new about accusations of racism against Satanism, and these dolts don't help matters any. Don't get me wrong, I have no objection to being hated by the herd. I do believe however, that if I am to be hated I should be hated for what I am, not for what I am not.

Some time ago I was approached by a man who had heard me talking about the detrimental effect that the welfare system was having on society. This man then handed me a piece of paper. I looked at it and found that it was a membership application for the Klan. I told this moron that I was not what he thought I was, and that he had obviously misunderstood my position. I also told him that I had about as much use for him and his idiotic kind as I did for the masses of welfare collectors.

To make it perfectly clear, the KKK is a Christian organization. Their applications even require you to attest to being both Christian and Aryan. Yes, Satanists want to see the end of the welfare system. We do not oppose only the helping of blacks; we oppose the helping of all races. The weak and stupid should be allowed to perish, not just weak and stupid blacks. We are not racists. We want to see the strong and intelligent of all races prevail.

Anton LaVey has said that Satanism is concerned with ethic, not ethnic. The following is a statement by Dr. LaVey taken from an interview in the RE/Search publication, *Modern Primitives*:

> "My most elitist, Satanic society dream is of something that's not based on racism, but based on intelligence vs. stupidity—that's all! There are the stupid and there are the intelligent. There are people that are alive and vital

and sensitive and thinking, and there are the people who are the dead, the cloned, the pods that are just things. They're the ones that I feel should be put to the flame-thrower, regardless of race."

TAKING THE CHRIST OUT OF CHRISTMAS

Well folks, it's that time of year again. Once more we are bombarded with Christian propaganda—disgusting homilies on forgiveness, empty babble about peace, and exhortations to put aside the "merely material" aspects of the holidays and to remember that it is, after all, Jesus' birthday. Well, the time has come to burst their bubble. What they call Christmas has been around a lot longer than the Jesus myth has.

From time immemorial people have been celebrating the winter solstice, the rebirth of the sun (not the son). In ancient Rome they had a celebration known as Saturnalia. This was a week-long revel in honor of Mithras. The end of the festivities came on December twenty-fifth, the day on which it was said that Mithras was born of a virgin. Bear in mind that the cult of Mithras predates the Jesus myth by some four hundred and fifty years, nor is Mithras the only such mythological figure. Many of the symbols associated with Christmas also have a pre-Christian origin. The Christmas tree is symbolic of Yggdrasill, the world tree of Norse mythology. Holly and mistletoe were held sacred by the druids. The tradition of kissing under the mistletoe can be viewed as a summoning forth of lust. The modern nativity scene had its parallel in ancient Egyptian representations of the infant Horus attended by his mother Isis and his foster father Seb. Even Santa Claus has his pagan counterpart. In ancient Greece there was a festival called the anthesteria in which trees were decorated, children were given gifts and Dionysus came to town in a sleigh. So the next time someone says it's time to put the Christ back in Christmas, tell them he never belonged there in the first place.

I remember when I was young, I always used to laugh at those people who would put on their most pious faces and babble about peace on Earth, goodwill towards man and all those other clichés of the season. Every year much is made of this, and Christians actually go so far as to say that Jesus brought peace to the world. I realize that their self-imposed ignorance blinds Christians, but I cannot see how even the most blissfully ignorant can truly believe such a blatant and bald-faced lie. How many people have been killed in wars since the Christian era began, and how many have been killed in the name of Christ? Prince of peace? Yeah, right.

Let's look at their Christ in the cold, hard light of twentieth century reality, shall we? Most people don't give a damn about the pallid Christ. He might receive lip service, but that's about it. Christmas is a festival of greed; in fact, I like to call it Mammonsmas. Everybody thinks about what they will get. Should anyone object that the reason people get things is because they are given as gifts, how much do you suppose people would get if they gave nothing? People give only when they expect to get in return. Santa Claus has long since replaced Jesus as the symbolic focus of the holidays. And why is that? It is because Santa Claus is the bearer of gifts. Yes, I know there are the injunctions toward being good or you will receive no gifts, but this is not so much a moral injunction as it is a means of obtaining well-mannered children—a goal sought by parents of all kinds.

I have shown that the religious aspects of Christmas predate Christianity by at least four hundred and fifty years, that the symbols associated with Christmas all have their pagan analogs, and that Jesus was hardly the first such mythological savior figure in history. I have further shown that in our present society the Christmas holiday is dominated by the figure of Santa Claus, and not Christ, and that the whole focus of Christmas is on gifts—not gift-giving as people like to think, but gift-getting, for as I have said people give that they may get. Now don't get me wrong. I am not criticizing the materialistic focus of the Christmas season, only the hypocritical Christian bullshit that fills the air with its noxious perfumery.

I say let's call a spade a spade and recognize once and for all that Christ has about as much to do with Christmas as Christopher Columbus had to do with discovering the North American continent: *none at all!*

THE LION & THE CHILD

In *Thus Spake Zarathustra*, Friedrich Nietzsche tells the story of the three metamorphoses. The basic idea is that mankind will undergo three metamorphoses; these three stages, the Camel, the Lion, and the Child are metaphoric representations depicting the attributes common to each. The Camel represents the respecter of tradition, the Christian type. The Camel seeks burdens to bear; it carries the weight of past tradition. The Lion is the next phase. The Lion throws off the Camel's burdens and seeks to be its own master. The Lion must fight a Dragon on whose scales are written "Thou Shalt". The Dragon represents the traditions that the Camel served. When the Dragon is destroyed the Lion undergoes the final transformation: it becomes the Child. The Child represents the superman, it writes its own laws, and serves no master. We are all familiar with the Camel, and as its time has passed I will not discuss it any further. As I said, this story is a parable about the human race, but it is also possible to interpret it in a more personal way, and that is what I'm going to do.

I assume that everyone who is reading this has reached at least the Lion state. After all, you probably wouldn't be reading this if you were still following the Camel's path. The most important thing for the Lions to know is that you must not fight the Dragon on its terms. If you do fight it that way you will be weakened, while at the same time you will strengthen the Dragon. The end result is that you may very well revert to a Camel state, or remain locked in the Lion state. This reversion to the Camel may appear at first to be Lion-like but close observation will reveal that it is very conformist. As Satanists we must not continue to fight our Dragons forever. We must not merely reject the ways of the herd, we must go our own way, create our own laws. The Lion cannot do this; it is pure iconoclasm, a destroyer. Only the Child can create. Now I am going to discuss the idea in terms of how those who have destroyed their own Dragons must deal with a world where Dragons still exist.

Since the Child represents creation, we must retain at least some aspects of the Lion nature; in effect we must be were-lions, ever ready to carry the attack to such Dragons as we meet. Just as the Child state can only come to the race when the Dragon has been destroyed, we cannot wholly forsake our Lion natures until the last Dragon to plague mankind has been defeated. To be honest though, I don't believe that that day will ever come. There will always be Dragons.

LAW & ORDER

In 1967 Anton LaVey set down the Eleven Satanic Rules of the Earth. These rules summarize briefly the true law—Lex Talionis, the law of the claw. These rules are the basis for a workable and Satanic system of law. This system would establish order, rather than protect the weak. If you were to attempt to summarize the current system of law in this society in such a way it would probably run closer to being eleven volumes than eleven rules. For any who have not read the Rules of the Earth I have copied them below.

1. Do not give opinions or advice unless you are asked.
2. Do not tell your troubles to others unless you are sure that they want to hear them.
3. When in another's lair, show him respect or else do not go there.
4. If a guest in your lair annoys you, treat him cruelly and without mercy.
5. Do not make sexual advances unless you are given the mating signal.
6. Do not take that which does not belong to you unless it is a burden to the other person and he cries out to be relieved.
7. Acknowledge the power of magic if you have employed it successfully to obtain your desires. If you deny the power of magic after having called upon it with success, you will lose all you have obtained.
8. Do not complain about anything to which you need not subject yourself.
9. Do not harm little children.
10. Do not kill non-human animals unless attacked or for your food.
11. When walking in open territory, bother no one. If someone bothers you, ask him to stop. If he does not stop, destroy him.

Periodically there is much talk of legal reform. Until a recognition of these basic principles is made, there can be no viable reform of the legal system. Rather than waste our time, energy and resources housing and "rehabilitating" criminals, destroy them. Rather than hounding those who are only violating moral codes, and harming no one, destroy the parasites that suck away the life-blood of society and give nothing in return. It is time to start anew. Throw out the old law, and bring in the new. The Rules of the Earth shall provide the foundation. Let the weak and the wretched be swept aside. Hail the strong! Hail the law!—Lex Satanicus. In the *Hymn to the Satanic Empire* Dr LaVey wrote a verse that states the facts simply and eloquently, it is: *"Even though tricksters make the law, Justice is served by fang and claw"*

DEMOCRACY

Contrary to popular belief there is a state religion in the United States, and no I'm not talking about Christianity. The state religion in the good old U.S.A. is democracy. Just like the emperor worship of imperial Rome, the cult of democracy doesn't care what other religion you practice as long as you pay the token reverence to the *sacred* institutions of democracy. Satanists therefore constitute a double threat since we are not only in opposition to the majority religion; we also reject the cornerstone of democratic ideology—the idea that all men are equal.

The cult of democracy has many gods and demigods. Among those gods are Abraham Lincoln, Franklin Roosevelt, John Kennedy and "The Common Man". There are also many devils, the greatest of these is probably Adolf Hitler, but there are many others. The priests of this religion are politicians, and the nine Justices of the Supreme Court are the oracles of those highest and holiest gods, the Founding Fathers, but those founders would not have wanted to be deified. If they could see what has evolved from what they started, I'm sure they would be horrified. For the most part these men were thoughtful and intelligent. Their great mistake was a far too idealistic assessment of human nature. This false assessment of humanity is based on the assumption that all men are created equal, or at least have equal potential for self-rule. The entire structure of democracy is based on this idea; remove it, and the entire house of cards will collapse. Those who believe in the egalitarian pipe-dream are bound to think of democracy as the ideal form of government. We understand that not only are all men not equal, the majority of humans are invariably inferior examples of the species. Those who recognize this fact see democracy as a horrible thing.

In the early years of the United States an intellectual aristocracy ran the nation. It was far from perfect, but I think that this nation would be far better off if this situation had lasted. Unfortunately, when the first generation raised on the poisonous doctrine of equality came of age they rejected this aristocracy in favor of the "Common Man". The rabble found a leader to rally around with Andrew Jackson. Jackson was a soldier from the wilds of Tennessee with the white trash's virulent hatred of the southern aristocracy. Today it is generally argued that the American Civil War was fought over the issue of states' rights, or over slavery. These were merely pretexts. The true goal of the American Civil War was to destroy the last bastion of the aristocratic ideal.

Democracy, by its very nature, must degenerate into mob rule. The Scottish historian Alexander Tytler said, "A democracy cannot exist as a permanent form of government. It can only exist until a majority of voters discover that they can vote themselves largess out of the public treasury." This has already happened.

Democracy was born from a sense that the established forms of government were no longer effective. Just as the old feudal kingdoms evolved into monarchies based on the idea of Divine Right, democracy has evolved into a cult. It is widely believed that democracy is inviolable. It is thought that any suggestion that the government cannot be corrected from within is unconscionable, but as Satanists we know that "no human ideal standeth sure." This puts us in a unique position. Democracy is a failure and is doomed to fall. If we are prepared, we will survive its fall as conquerors. If not, we will perish with it. It is time to dethrone the common man and restore an aristocracy of the elite.

WHO SAID WHAT?

It is commonly believed that Satanism encourages all sorts of despicable activities, such as animal or human sacrifice, rape, murder or self-mutilation, or that people under the influence of Satanic ideas open themselves up to possession by external entities. Any objective reading of *The Satanic Bible* will show that these accusations are plainly ridiculous, but what about the Christian's bible? Below I will reproduce a selection of bible passages that will clearly show that Christianity advocates all of these practices in their own bible. I am not making any effort to be comprehensive here. There are numerous passages that I did not choose to copy down.

> *Leviticus 8:15.* And he slew it (a bull in this case); and Moses took the blood, and put it upon the horns of the altar round about with his finger, and purified the altar, and poured the blood at the bottom of the altar.

> *Leviticus 8:30.* And Moses took the anointing oil, and of the blood which was upon the altar, and sprinkled it upon Aaron and upon his garments and upon his sons, and upon his son's garments with him.

> *Numbers 31:17-18.* Now therefore kill every male among the little ones, and kill every woman that hath known man by lying with him. But all the women children that have not known a man by lying with him, keep alive for yourselves.

> *Matthew 18:7-9.* Woe to that man by whom offense cometh. Wherefore if thy hand or thy foot offend thee, cut them off, and cast them from thee; it is better for thee to enter into life halt or maimed rather than having two hands or two feet to be cast into everlasting fire. And if

thine eye offend thee, pluck it out, and cast it from thee; it is better for thee to enter into life with one eye, rather than having two eyes to be cast into eternal fire.

Galatians 2:20. I live; yet not I, but Christ liveth in me.

Phillipians 1:21. To live is Christ, to die is gain.

Many Christians probably don't know that these passages exist because they don't spread that cheery peace and love pap that is so popular with the masses. Even if they have seen them, they don't think about what they are saying. These six passages endorse self mutilation, a love of death, a desire to lose oneself to external influence, animal sacrifice, smearing blood on priests, infanticide, murder, genocide, and sexual slavery of young girls.

I trust that every reader of this article is familiar with *The Satanic Bible* so I won't go into what it says, but ask yourself who is saying what?

A PACK OF LIES, AND A DECLARATION OF WAR

Recently I was looking through a stack of used books and came across a copy of Carl A. Raschke's *Painted Black*. I'd heard about this book before and I had intended to do a review of it in this issue. I decided not to do that because the book was worse than I thought it would be—in fact, I couldn't finish it. I threw it aside after seventy pages and later went back and referred to the index to read a few select passages.

In the first chapter the author discusses the Matamoros killings. The Matamoros drug cult is alternately referred to as Palo-Mayombe, Santeria, Satanism or a resurgence of the Aztec religion. The author even tries to draw connections to Buddhism. In the author's rather limited mind all of these things are synonymous. Later the author implies that only Judeo-Christian religions are real religions with all of the others merely convenient fronts for criminal activity. Anton LaVey's *Politically Incorrect Manifesto* addresses this sort of thing. If any of you haven't read this yet I can't recommend it highly enough.

In the second chapter the author goes into a murder in Joplin Missouri. This case was also featured on the infamous Geraldo debacle. The basic facts of this case are as follows. A teenage boy is killed and thrown down a well. This boy was one of several such boys who used and sold drugs. (The author mentions that there is some evidence that the dead one was stealing both money and drugs from the rest, but he apparently considers this unimportant.) These drug-addled morons were dabblers in a hodgepodge of occultism and heavy metal style pseudo-Satanism. By calling this drug-related gang murder a sacrifice these kids were able to blame their crimes on Satanism in order to avoid any responsibility for their actions. The author himself even testified at one of the trials that, because of their involvement in "Satanism," the killers couldn't help themselves. One of the killers had apparently read *The Satanic Bible*, and the author makes much of his professed devotion to Dr. LaVey. What Mr. Raschke neglects to mention is that this boy and his comrades consistently acted in a way that was contrary to the true Satanic doctrine set forth by Dr. LaVey. While the author is quick to point a blaming finger at Anton LaVey, rather than at the actual murderers, at no time does he ask where the good Christian parents of these juvenile delinquents were. How can a responsible parent not know when their child is using or selling drugs? Once again, the herd seeks to avoid responsibility through a convenient scapegoat. The fact that such worthless vermin have read *The Satanic Bible* is irrelevant. The fact is that, even if they've read it, these cretins obviously didn't understand or apply it. It is probably as far beyond their capacity to understand the principles of Satanism as iron smelting is beyond the capacity of a colony of ants.

The author briefly goes into the history of the "World Satanic Conspiracy." It is said that Anton LaVey was chosen to lead the World Satanic Movement in 1960. Previous leaders included Aleister Crowley and Eliphas Levi. Later in the book the author has apparently changed his mind after talking to Michael Aquino, and believes that Dr. LaVey is no more than a carnival huckster out for a quick buck. Well, which is it? Is he the shadowy grand master of the Satanic criminal underground, or carny con man?

The book is full of such contradictions and blatant lies. At one point the author suggests that Satanists should be required to register with the government, and should be placed under government surveillance. What is readily apparent is that this book is a desperate attack from a dying movement. The Christians are fond of saying that the Christian church is the body of Christ. From my perspective, Christianity is the bloated and stinking corpse of their god. A putrescent mass of corruption, and I say that it's high time that it was buried.

PERSECUTION

If you listen to Christians you will get the impression that they are being persecuted for their religious beliefs. If you look at the facts you will see that what is really going on is that Christians do not get all of what they want, do not get their way all the time, and this to them constitutes persecution. It is truly a shame that these whiny Christian bastards don't take to heart this command from their precious Jesus—"Count it all joy when you are persecuted." Maybe if they did they would shut up. Just as their claims of persecution in the present day do not hold up, the popular notion that the Roman Empire tried to systematically destroy the Christian religion is also untrue.

Following the burning of Rome in 64 CE, the emperor Nero did blame the fire on the Christians, and did put some to death and harass the others. Even if the Christians did not start the fire, which is unknown, the subsequent attacks upon them were almost inevitable. They were the perfect scapegoats—an unpopular minority that openly shunned the values of Roman society, an ignorant rabble claiming to be the sole bearers of truth. To make things even more perfect, the Christians would not resist. Most examples of alleged persecution in the early era of the Christian church were generally one of two things:

A) Legal actions against Christians for disorderly conduct of various sorts.

B) Massacres of obnoxious Christian missionaries by those who didn't want to be converted.

I am basing this statement on the fact that contemporary Roman documents speak of rioting Christians, and on an observation of modern Christian behavior. If a modern Christian cries persecution when he is arrested for vandalizing an abortion clinic, it is reasonable to assume that early Christians would do the same when arrested for violating a temple or disrupting rites of the pagan majority. Similarly, if Christians today feel that they have a duty to tell every non-Christian that god, in his infinite mercy, is going to fling us all into eternal fire if we don't repent, the early Christians probably did the same. It doesn't surprise me that these obnoxious creatures were often killed by those they approached.

The idea that the Roman empire of the first and second centuries of the Christian era deliberately sought to stamp out Christianity is ridiculous. The pagans of classical antiquity were noted for their religious tolerance, and the Roman Empire was no exception. Anyone who looks at the diverse cults that existed side by side, not only in the provinces but also in Rome herself, must see that such a charge is utterly unfounded. Only among Jews and Christians could you find the level of religious bigotry that is needed for true religious persecution. Between these two groups, each claiming the favor of *the one true God,* there was considerable friction and I have no doubt that if there was any persecution of Christians in this period that it was the Jews, not the Romans, who were behind it.

The only long-term *persecution* of Christians by the empire was not a religious matter at all, at least not directly. These persecutions were, like those of Nero, politically motivated. During the third century CE there was a great deal of dissension in the empire. In some ways it corresponds to the multiculturalism of today. In an effort to restore a sense of unity in the empire, the emperor Decius, in the year 250 CE, reinstated the observance of the state cult. At this time everyone was required to offer sacrifice to the state gods, notably the emperors. Those who refused were subject to exile and their wealth could be confiscated. The Christians were not singled out as victims by this law; they simply refused to obey the law. This situation persisted until the end of Diocletian's reign in 305 CE

In contrast to this, from Gratian's law of 382 CE, which limited pagans in their right to perform their rites and ceremonies to Justinian's laws of 529 that made being a pagan, Jew or Christian heretic punishable by death, there was an ever-increasing level of persecution directed at non-Christians. Temples, idols and books destroyed. Roving gangs of monks forced conversion on people. Rioting by the Christian rabble became commonplace. Here began the dark ages.

It is tempting to think of Christianity as the cause of Rome's fall, but this is untrue. Christianity found a foothold in Rome only because of the sickness already endemic in Roman society. Christianity is a pestilence that gained access to Rome through its decadence and spread like a cancer. Had the patrician class been able to hold out against Christianity, and confined it to the rabble, the dark ages might have been avoided. It was through its contamination of Rome that Christianity got into the otherwise vital and healthy cultures that were arising in northern Europe. The taint of Christianity put its indelible mark on them, twisting them into its own image. Christianity sickened these societies and that is a crime it has not answered for. Who can say what these societies might have become had Christianity not infected them in their infancy?

AN ANSWER TO URBAN BLIGHT

During the rioting in L.A. in the wake of the Rodney King verdict there was a great deal of discussion about the underlying causes of it. In all their talk about injustice, poverty and drugs they failed to notice the true reason. Aside from the generally poor breeding prevalent in the cities, a widespread sense of victimization is the principal cause. At all levels of society people have come to regard themselves as victims. The more victimized you feel you are, the more you will resent others. In the cities many groups of self-proclaimed victims compete for sympathy and thus resent each other. When this resentment comes to a head, rioting breaks out. The obvious solution would be to follow in the footsteps of Vlad Tepes, and invite all of these *victims* to a party and burn down the hall. That's not going to happen anytime soon though. A change must come in how such rabble are governed.

An iron handed aristocracy is needed—an aristocracy that isn't afraid to rule. Time and again history has shown that as long as the rulers of a nation actually rule there is little fear of upheaval from below. Whenever these rulers show weakness and indecision though, the mob will rise against them. Our *rulers* are weak. Despite the protestations of many so-called experts, the people would trade away any voice in the government for a benevolent aristocracy that gave them stability, order and a sense of belonging. The vast majority of people are manifestly unfit for self rule. Any attempt to force it upon them serves nobody's best interests. The solution to the problem of the cities doesn't lie in giving the underclass a say in their destiny, nor should their worthless existence be subsidized for some ridiculous humanitarian reason. Only the relentless application of natural law at all levels will bring about an ultimate solution. The herd must be thinned. An aristocracy of wolves is needed to carry out that task.

KILL A COW FOR SATAN?

In Alabama the yokels have been stirred up of late over a series of "cattle mutilations". At first the papers fed the fires of ignorance and hysteria with stories of Satanists in helicopters swooping down on unsuspecting and helpless cattle with surgical instruments and pumps to siphon off the blood. Later they acknowledged that it was probably something as mundane as coyotes, which exist in abundance in the area. "Coincidentally" the papers stopped playing blame the Satanists after I contacted them to illuminate them on the history of "cattle mutilation". It's quite understandable to me why the papers would try to blow it up into something more than it is since "Coyotes kill local cows" isn't exactly a captivating headline.

Predictably, the ignorant hayseeds were not pacified by the revelation that coyotes are the most likely culprits. There are still a few, mostly fundamentalist Christians, who still believe that Satanists are behind it all, especially since a few goats turned up dead—everybody *knows* that we just *love* to kill goats—but most of them now believe that it was either a government conspiracy, a covert research project to see if power lines cause cancer, or flying saucers.

The "mutilations" followed the classic pattern. The ears, "lips", belly, and internal organs removed with little blood at the scene. There was one exception to the pattern; a bull whose penis was removed, but this was almost certainly done so as to make a walking stick of it. If you tell these half wits that this is the classic pattern of coyote predation they will look at you as though you were an idiot. They assume that since a man's first inclination is to eat the muscle rather than the soft external parts and viscera that a coyote would share that inclination. Furthermore, they assume that since a man with no special tools would make a mess in the process of killing and disemboweling a cow, that all predators are equally inept.

I suppose it is inevitable that these people would be reluctant to accept so mundane an explanation as coyotes. After all, this is the biggest thing to happen in their drab little lives. To be totally honest, I'm surprised that they haven't suggested that werewolves are to blame. Maybe they will yet.*

* *Author's note*—In the weeks following the original publication of this piece a woman did in fact call the police to report a werewolf in her back yard. This werewolf proved to be a vagrant with long & unkempt beard & hair.

GIVE ME THAT OLD TIME RELIGION

Recently I read something about a group of American Indians who want to restore their old religion that it would be restored to the purity it had before the tribes were conquered. There is a similar sentiment conveyed in much Neo-Pagan material. I do not dispute the idea that there was much in some strains of pagan thought that is praiseworthy, but the idea that we should return to a pre-Christian system is silly. What is needed is not a return to a pre-Christian way, but rather a progression to a post-Christian system.

The Neo-Pagans of today are almost invariably living in the past. They seek to follow their traditions, all the while ignoring the fact that those traditions were developed centuries ago. Many times these people will argue against Christianity by saying that it is derived from an alien culture that has nothing to do with them. This is indisputably true, but these same people will then go to perform some ritual dedicated to an imagined neolithic mother goddess, or go to their favorite grove and perform pseudo-druidical rites (since we have no reliable written records of the rites of the druids, nor any genuinely surviving druid tradition it is ridiculous to claim to be a druid), or attend some Odinist religious ceremony. What does this have to do with their culture? They are as far removed from the neolithic age, the heyday of the Celts or the Viking era as they are from the Jewish near east of two thousand years ago. As much as you might like to play *"Let's pretend Christianity didn't win"* it is impossible. Christianity won and destroyed the old pagan religions, which is just as well because the world they were made for was swept away. The vestiges of these old religions, which the modern day pagans cling to, are the mummified scraps and tatters of dead religions.

Neo-Pagans will go on interminably about how Satanism is merely the flip-side of Christianity. This proves that they know nothing about us. We wear Satan's name because all of those admirable pagan values that Christianity rejected are equated with

Satan in the minds of the Christian majority. Only Satanism has taken from these pagan sources that which is still vital and applicable in the modern world and integrated it into a living philosophy and religion. Others seek to go back to a time before the Christian pestilence was unleashed on the west. Only Satanism dares look to a time when this triumph of the worthless is forgotten.

The old ways are for the past; the old religions are for the dead.

THE CHURCH OF THE PASSED BUCK

The cult of dysfunctionalism is alive and well in the world today. Everywhere you turn you will find someone who blames his or her shortcomings on a less than perfect childhood. Once, these people would have been looked upon with contempt, but no more. Not only are they not condemned for trying to shift responsibility for their flaws onto parents or teachers, they are actually praised for "coming to grips" with their problems. The idea has taken hold that if you suffer some childhood trauma, no matter how benign, that you will be psychically scarred for life—that you are helpless before your fate. According to the modern gospel of dysfunctionalism, the children of alcoholics will grow up to be alcoholics themselves, the victims of pedophiles shall likewise become pedophiles etc., etc. There is however a way to end this cycle—an extensive (and, I might add, expensive) period of therapy, sometimes a lifetime of it.

I am certainly not trying to make light of the damage that can be done to a child's mind through such things as pedophilia, but I believe that children are far more resilient than they are thought to be. It should be obvious to anyone why such ideas are so popular. First, the psychiatric industry makes millions through books, lectures and therapy; second, because they excuse irresponsibility.

A common example of the kind of idiocy that is routinely discussed in this matter is wife beating. Hundreds of women remain with abusive husbands, and all of them expect, or demand, our sympathy. No doubt some of these women are, in reality, masochists who enjoy the abuse. But most of them, despite their complaining, enjoy the sympathy and attention that they receive and feel that it's worth it to stay and get hit every now and then. I have no compassion for such women. If they truly wanted out, they know where the door is. Surely they are not all chained to the wall when their husbands leave the house.

Another fairly common occurrence these days is for someone

to suddenly *"remember"* horrible situations of abuse some twenty or thirty years after the fact. Oddly enough, these people don't ever remember these things until a hypnotherapist with an axe to grind begins to *"treat"* them. A perfect example of this is detailed in the book *Michelle Remembers.*

Poor Michelle had problems. She went to see a psychiatrist and under hypnosis *"remembered"* being ritually abused by Satanists (and Satan too for that matter). The fact that this psychiatrist was also a Roman Catholic missionary was surely just a coincidence. Despite an overwhelming lack of any sort of evidence such people are generally believed. After all, why would they lie about such things?

Sometimes it seems to me that there is a twelve step program for everything these days. One day there will be a twelve step program to wean you off of twelve step programs. There can be no doubt that these programs are in fact a religion, and that these twelve steps are, in fact, a new apostle's creed. For those of you who are unfamiliar with them, these are the twelve steps:

1. admit your powerlessness
2. believe in a god (higher power)
3. turn your life over to god
4. make a moral inventory
5. confess your "sins"
6. want god to fix things
7. ask god to fix things
8. be willing to make amends
9. make amends ("I'm sorry, I couldn't help it.")
10. continue to confess your "sins"
11. pray
12. spread the faith.

It sounds like the same old poison that the west has put up with for the last 2,000 years to me. There's not enough difference in Christianity and the twelve steps to cover this sheet of paper, yet hundreds, perhaps thousands of people will be ordered by law to enroll in these programs every year.

Typically these people who have lived through such things are called survivors (e.g. incest survivors). They may have survived, but they haven't overcome these problems. They dwell upon these things so much that they become one with them. They may be surviving but they are not living. Once, such people would have been given a sort of grace period of indulgence to overcome a trauma, but eventually they'd have been told to get over it and get on with their lives. Now they are encouraged to nurture their *"wounded inner child"*. Well, it's time for all those wounded inner children to grow up. The hero of this age is a neurotic ex-junkie who goes on a talk show to cry about how his father never said "I love you" to him.

Perhaps the greatest danger of such an ideology is the damage done when a society begins to see victimization as a virtue. When a society lavishes all of its attention on whoever cries the most it is not surprising that ever increasing numbers of people will come to see themselves as irreparably damaged victims. The dysfunctionalism movement is the consummation of Judeo-Christian decadence.

There is no denying the fact that we are all shaped by influences and experiences beyond our control, and that no one's will is absolutely free, but until people are held accountable for their own actions there is no escaping the downward spiral we are locked into. It could be said that John Wayne Gacy was, because of his life experiences, unable to keep from sodomizing and killing young boys. Perhaps so, but that doesn't matter in the least. Is a homicidal pedophile more acceptable just because he is so warped that he couldn't help himself? I don't think so. I make no moral judgment of the man's acts, none is needed. If a rabid dog attacked you you'd destroy it. It wouldn't matter to you that the dog was sick, and couldn't help it. Just as you hold a mad dog responsible for biting you, so you should hold people accountable for their actions no matter what kind of sob story they have to tell. Currently the trend is to pass the buck to someone else. It is time for everyone to say that, as regards their own actions, the buck stops here.

POLITICS

> *Every national appeal is now made, not to the noblest and best, but to the riff-raff, the slave hordes, who possess less intelligence than night owls. All that is brave, honorable, heroic is ignored tacitly for fear of offending the deified herd—the majority.*
>
> —RAGNAR REDBEARD

Every four years Americans are treated to a spectacle of profound idiocy—the presidential election. The candidates, in their mad dash to placate the mob, will endure great indignities because if there is anything that the rabble cannot abide it is someone with an innate sense of dignity. The two main candidates are at present (1992 CE) arguing about who represents "traditional values". Whose traditional values are they talking about? The values of the ignorant masses of course. You can clearly see who the politicians are pandering to from the fact that the word "elite" is being used as an epithet with which to attack their opponents. At one point the idea of rule by plebiscite was put forward, although no one took it very seriously except the mob. In a way, while it would create chaos, such mob rule would ultimately be a good thing since it would rapidly hasten the fall of the present system.

Recently I came across a statement by one of the Justices of the Supreme Court which criticized the court for refusing to yield to the demands of the Christian right and outlaw abortion. In this statement the Justice claimed that the court was increasingly conforming to what he characterized as a Nietzschean vision. I beg to differ with the Justice's assessment. I can see nothing in the U.S. government that even remotely resembles any of Nietzsche's ideas. On the contrary, when one reads Nietzsche's condemnations of the Reich you cannot help seeing the parallels with the U.S. government. Similarly in the Americans of the present day there is a clear resemblance to the shallow, stupid and boorish Germans that Nietzsche had so little regard for.

Ultimately a democracy is only as strong as its average citizen. The democracy of ancient Athens was a weak state. When it began, the heroic ideal was still fairly strong. It wasn't long though before those ideals began the rapid process of erosion that would lead to Greece's decline as a power. Not until the rise of Alexander would Greece again be a force to be reckoned with. How much weaker would a democracy founded upon the principle of egalitarianism be? The egalitarian ideal, with its continual leveling downwards, leads to a constantly lowering standard and with it, a rising tide of mediocrity.

For two centuries the U.S. has put up with such a mob placating, egalitarian democracy. It is high time that this wretched system be swept aside.

THE DEBT OF THE WEST?

I once heard it said that the west owed its culture to the contributions of the Jews, through Christianity. There were two notable contributions which, it was said, were behind all of the west's cultural advances. These two ideas were the bad conscience, and the sense of being the "Chosen People". To bad conscience was attributed the drive to excellence, while the sense of being *"chosen"* gave the west a sense of purpose and destiny. It was further argued that since both of these things derived from Judaic monotheism that had the west not rejected paganism that it would have stagnated and died. This entire argument is ludicrous!

I believe that most of the positive elements of western culture are derived from a primarily Greco-Roman or Germano-Celtic source and not a Judeo-Christian one. As I see it, bad conscience led only to a sense of guilt. It lies behind every puritanical repression and inquisition but not behind the pursuit of excellence. Look to classical antiquity. Were not the ancient Greeks driven in the pursuit of excellence? Did not the Romans feel a sense of duty driving them on, without the negativity of the bad conscience? What of the sense of being "The Chosen People"? Has it not always been the justification of narrow mindedness, ignorance and bigotry? Didn't Alexander feel a sense of purpose and destiny? Did Rome lack such an idea? Yet they weren't possessed of the petty bigotry of the Jews or Christians.

There is no denying that Judeo-Christian values have heavily influenced western culture but western virtues have survived in spite of these influences, not because of them. Judeo-Christianity is a parasite that has, for centuries, drained the vitality of the west. It has taken all it could grasp, and perverted all it has touched but it has given absolutely nothing of value to the west... Nothing!

A POISONOUS *"TREAT"*

For years, one of the most popular of the urban legends was the widespread agitation that some sick individuals pass out poisoned candy on Halloween. I came upon just such a poisonous treat which some child had the good sense to throw away. This "treat" is a small propaganda pamphlet produced by the Faith, Prayer & Tract League of Grand Rapids Michigan. This little piece of filth was distributed to children in lieu of candy by a group of sick individuals who are collectively known as Christians. Nietzsche called Christians sick animals. If you had any doubts about how sick they are, the text of this monstrous tract should allay those doubts. This is the text of the tract which is entitled *The Best Treat*:

> "What is the best treat you got in your trick or treat bag? A piece of candy? Candy tastes good, but in a few minutes it's all gone. What if someone put a dollar bill in your bag? Would you throw it away because it is only paper? What would be the best treat if you were blind or crippled? Wouldn't you be thrilled if in your bag you found a piece of paper telling you about a doctor who could cure you? Well, that's what this piece of paper is! We want to tell you something that is worth more than all the candy in the world. That good news is that there is Someone who can cure you of your worst sickness the sickness of your soul. Maybe you didn't even know you were sick? But you know that you're not always happy. You know that people do mean things to you. You know that you are naughty. All bad things are called sin. Big people sin, but so do children. This is the sickness of our souls. Jesus loves boys and girls. He wants to cure them of this sickness. Jesus is God, but He came to earth long ago as a baby. (We call His birthday Christmas) Later He died to pay for our sins so that everybody who believes on Him

> will be happier now—and will live forever! Isn't that wonderful? Be sure to learn more about Jesus! Boys and girls can learn about Jesus from their parents or in church or Sunday school. The *Bible* tells us about Him. To know Jesus as your savior and friend is the most important thing in the world. That's why we hope that this little paper will be the best treat that you got this Halloween!"

Disgusting isn't it? It's bad enough that these bastards pollute the minds of their own children with their insidious doctrines of collective guilt, but to take advantage of a joyful occasion, one of the few festivals that the Christians have not yet tainted with their morbid philosophy, to attempt to poison the minds of the children of others is truly disgusting. Anyone that is sick enough to do such a thing should be tortured to death. This tract proves beyond a shadow of a doubt who the real Halloween child poisoners are, because if the ideas set forth in this vile tract are not poisonous I don't know what is.

SHALL WE GIVE THANKS?

With the onset of winter, the nauseating "Christmas season" comes upon us. Slipping in, almost unnoticed in all the hype, comes the indigenous American holiday—Thanksgiving. While there isn't as much hype about it this holiday is every bit as disgusting as Christmas, in its implications anyway. This isn't terribly surprising since it originated amongst the puritans, as disgusting a collection of humanity as has ever been assembled.

Like Christmas, there is little in the modern observance of Thanksgiving of its pious origins. If Christmas is now a festival of greed, Thanksgiving is a festival of gluttony. If these holidays were observed as such there would be no problem. The problem lies in the disgusting layer of pious hypocrisy that is laid over them. Each year the story of the first thanksgiving is retold with an exhortation to give thanks for all we have been given.

Speaking for myself, I've been given precious little, and when I have received a gift I have thanked the giver at the time. Why wait until the end of November? The traditional way of celebrating Thanksgiving is to put an expensive feast on the table, and give thanks to god for providing it. If I put on such a feast, do I not pay for it myself? Why should I lessen myself by crediting all the things I have strived for to the benevolence of god? Some would say that it makes no difference what Thanksgiving means, or what its implications are. They simply see in it a good excuse to have a big dinner party. Why wait? Celebrate when you want, not when they say that it's acceptable. Christmas is a fallen holiday, and it can be rehabilitated. Thanksgiving however is tainted down to its core. The best thing to do with it is forget it. We don't need a celebration of puritanical self-loathing, and groveling before some imaginary god.

A FALLACIOUS FOUNDATION

"We hold these truths to be self evident, that all men are created equal, that they are endowed by their creator with certain unalienable rights, that among these are life, liberty and the pursuit of happiness."

These words open the second paragraph of the Declaration of Independence, which is often spoken of as one of histories greatest, and most profound documents. The masses often accept that idea without thinking about it (but then they seldom think at all) but is it really?

The first of these "self evident truths" is that all men are created equal. The modern interpretation of this is that all men are equal, but even if you take it at face value the statement is not only inaccurate, it's insulting. Look around you, are all people equal? Of course not. Go to any school and you will see that some children are superior to others. This demonstrates plainly that inequality is not something that comes into being with adulthood. Let's go even further back. Even infants show clear evidence that there is no equality. Equality does not exist at any level of human society. In order to put forth a facade of equality, assorted egalitarian measures have been implemented in an effort to level society; but as Edmund Burke noted, "Those who attempt to level, never equalize."

Hard on the heels of this falsehood comes another, the doctrine of unalienable rights—the idea that man is naturally due certain rights, and that it is the duty of society to safeguard these rights. There is no evidence that nature grants such rights, and even if it did, these so-called unalienable rights are violated every day as a matter of routine.

Look around at the natural world. If natural rights existed it would be reasonable to assume that you could find them in nature. The fact is, they aren't there. In nature, rights are determined by strength and intelligence. Nothing is born with any right, save the right to die if it shows itself unfit to live. This notion of natural rights derives in large part from the writings of Jean-Jacques Rousseau, an 18th century philosopher. Rousseau believed in the idea of the noble savage existing in a state of perfect innocence. Rousseau felt that all of man's ills, like inequality, were created by man and not inborn. In this sense, although he was an atheist, Rousseau believed in an edenic existence at the dawn of time from which mankind has fallen. This naive conception of nature was never taken seriously by those who had regular contact with nature beyond the protection of the cities, but even today there are those who think of primitive people as examples of unfallen men. Man did not fall. He started at the bottom, and has had to claw his way up from those modest beginnings. Nature did not endow him with natural rights, nor does it promise that what he has obtained he shall keep. In nature, might makes rights, and nature is stronger than man. Man therefore has only what nature has deigned to allow him. Through man's rejection of the dictates of nature he is in danger of being thrown back down to his beginnings.

The right to life is a concept much invoked by the Christian right these days, but it is violated every day. How many people will be murdered today? What of their unalienable right to life? The state will, at times, kill criminals. Is this not a violation of their natural right to life? It follows that if the taking of a human life was a violation of natural law, the act of murder would be fraught with dire consequences. Do such consequences arise naturally? No. The only consequences are culturally imposed. As a matter of fact, officially sanctioned killings are generally rewarded. If there is a single act that characterizes nature, it is killing. To suggest that nature has decreed an inborn right to life is laughable.

The right to liberty is the next on this list of absurdities. Go to any prison in the world and ask the inmates whether their right to liberty was unalienable. If you think that prisoners don't merit these innate rights, think about how many people will be held hostage. Does nature punish the violators of this right? Of course not, that's what the police are for. How many have become rich through the slave trade throughout history? Did nature punish these transgressors against *"natural law"*? No. If nature has a law regarding liberty it would read like this—You have the right to liberty until someone takes that liberty away. If you cannot maintain your freedom, nature doesn't promise that you can keep it.

The right to the pursuit of happiness is infringed upon constantly. The justification of this is generally called morality. Those who seek happiness in drug-induced states, those who pursue happiness in the beds of prostitutes, those who pursue happiness through gambling are all denied their natural right to the pursuit of happiness routinely. If you found a man who derived happiness through servitude, it would be unlawful for someone to grant him that happiness through enslaving him. Countless sexual acts are illegal in a nation built upon the notion that the right to pursue happiness is inborn. The hypocrisy of such an attitude is as sickening as the doctrine the hypocrisy arises from.

As we have seen, the so-called "Unalienable" rights mentioned at the beginning of this article are quite alienable. The idea that these rights derive from nature is entirely without support. In fact it is refuted by even a cursory look at nature. It is also clear that no one really takes these rights seriously, except to pay them lip service and enact token measures which only do harm by hindering the real natural laws. If it can be said that the Declaration of Independence is the foundation of not only the United States, but of all the western democracies, then that foundation is rotten. To establish a society built upon false principles is begging destruction. The central assumptions of modern western society are false. We are now tempting fate. If we do not rethink those false assumptions we will be destroyed. In the past the peoples of Europe were the conquerors of the world. Nature has no memory, and plays no favorites. The victories of the past do not ensure victories tomorrow. The adoption of the idiotic egalitarian pipe-dreams set down in the Declaration of Independence signaled a decline. To follow this course will only lead us to destruction.

EDUCATION

It is no secret that the educational system in this country is in decline. While almost everyone recognizes the problem almost nobody recognizes the reasons why. There is considerable effort to induce children to behave as a member of the group, and not as an individual. I read about a program which was to be tried in Alabama which is typical of the modern approach to education. In the program I read about, the children are placed in small study groups. No individual work is done. Everything revolves around "team-work". All grades are group grades. If anyone in a group is wrong then all members are penalized. This forces the intelligent to do all the work, and share the fruits of his labors with dullards who may well be illiterate, rather than risk being penalized for work done by others.

To force the intelligent children to drag around as baggage the mediocre or stupid children is to place an insurmountable obstacle before them. How many children will come to regard their superior intelligence as a curse because it obligates them to serve their inferiors? Such a system can only discourage learning. This sort of system, by catering to the mediocre and stupid is a positive reinforcement of mediocrity and stupidity. Such is always the problem of gearing everything to the lowest common denominator—the denominator will grow increasingly more common and lower all the time. By lowering standards to guarantee everyone a passing grade you make that passing grade meaningless. I will say this for this program: it is eminently well suited to producing welfare recipients.

Another element of this program is that each child is required to say something nice to everyone in the group. What if the child doesn't like everyone? Why push a child into the obsequious hypocrisy of the glad-hander? All this emphasis on socializing and group activity is another example of this society's headlong rush to go beyond the herd, and into the hive. The mind numbing conformity fostered by this system, the diminishing of individualistic values, the insistence that the only thing of value is collective effort, all are symptomatic of the problem in education today. Unfortunately, too many people in positions of authority think that they are a part of the solution.

REDEEMING THE COUNT

With the recent movie version of *Dracula*, Bram Stoker's immortal Count is in the midst of a resurgent popularity. If ever there were a Satanic archetype it is Dracula, and yet none of the many movies made about him have really done justice to that side of him. They have, for the most part, been content to portray him as a glorified leech, a mere parasite. I had hoped that this version would be better. It wasn't. In this article I will first look at the characters, as they appeared in the book, and then I will discuss the movie.

The novel, *Dracula*, can be seen as an allegory depicting the clash of two worlds. The protagonists represent the modern world with its democratic and egalitarian ideals. The Harkers are representatives of the rising middle-class. Simple, respectable people (a schoolteacher and a real-estate agent) of the sort who presume to rule the world. Arthur Holmwood is a member of the decaying aristocracy which is a pale shadow of the old aristocracy. Holmwood's kind are like the inbred and decadent *"royalty"* of today, the only kind of aristocracy the masses can tolerate. Dr. Seward, keeper of the local madhouse, is the priest of the new religion, science and medicine. Dr. VanHelsing acts as a bridge between the old religion and the new since he is equally at home with medicine and Christian metaphysics.

On the other side of the spectrum is Dracula himself. Dracula is the antithesis of Arthur Holmwood for he represents the old, strong, aristocracy. Dracula is also representative of an older order of humanity as well. Dracula is a predator who understands his place in the order of nature. A telling moment comes when Dracula refers to the howling of the wolves as music. Just as this reveals that Dracula is attuned to his own bestial nature, Harker's horrified response reveals his, and through him the modern age's, alienation from nature. Dracula's blend of animality, and the social graces further distances him from the masses. The mob can comprehend only simple either/or choices. Were he either an effete decadent, or a coarse brute he would be within their grasp, but as it is he is totally incomprehensible to them. This as much as anything causes the simple-minded masses to fear him.

There are two other characters who are both on the wrong side. Renfield, is like the weak minded simpletons who are always drawn to the majesty and power of the darkness. There is a lesson here for Satanists. The world is full of Renfields, and even though such people will slavishly serve and worship you they are ultimately unreliable. The other character I'm referring to is Quincey Morris. Morris represents that old American archetype of the rugged individualist. In *Dracula,* Morris has gotten himself caught up in the modern world, and its forces; a world he should reject rather than serve. It is significant that both Renfield and Morris die. Renfield was destroyed for his betrayal, while Morris is rewarded for his service by being allowed to die for the cause. It is the fate of those with misplaced loyalties that they must fall in the struggle.

The dichotomy presented in *Dracula* between the protagonists on the one hand, and Dracula on the other provides a good litmus test of where you fit in this clash of worlds. If your sympathies lie with Harker, VanHelsing and their ilk you are very likely to be in synch with the modern world. If you can empathize with Dracula though you are probably alienated from all that.

Now I'll go on to discuss the much ballyhooed movie. I cannot say that it was all bad. It is a beautiful movie to look at, and I also enjoyed the musical score. In fact, up until Dracula's arrival in England the movie is quite good. I found the introductory scene where Dracula renounces god and the church to be quite stirring. Unfortunately, from there things go downhill. Screenwriter James V. Hart wanted to humanize Dracula so he added two elements to the story. The first I have already mentioned. That is the scene which opens the movie wherein Dracula renounces the church which has betrayed him. The second element is what has torn the heart from the story. In this new variation on the story Dracula finds that Mina resembles his long dead wife and sets out to win her love once in England. To anyone who has read the book this is a ludicrous idea. I cannot imagine anyone who could actually like the character of Mina. Quite simply she is a shallow, stupid and tiresome woman. To suggest that Dracula could possibly love such a creature reveals how totally the people involved misunderstood the Count. In the book, Dracula "infects" Mina as an act of vengeance. As the vampire hunters are destroying his coffins, and defiling his lair Dracula slips past their guard to Mina's side. They stand by helplessly as he strikes them in the most painful way he could. With that act he turns the sweet taste of their apparent victory into a mouthful of ashes. In the movie, all that is lost. Coppola turns this consumate act of defiant vengeance into a sex scene.

The biggest problem is that Hart and Coppola are not philosophically suited to the material. It is truly ironic that the man who wrote that stirring opening sequence, and the man who filmed it are so incapable of understanding that it depicts a glorious, and heroic act of defiance and not an ignominious fall. They are both too strongly steeped in the whole Christian sin and redemption world view. They see Dracula as a lost soul in need of redemption. They see the grace of god as being vital. The Satanist knows that immortality does not come through faith in a crucified madman, or in the absolution of priests. Immortality is won through the defiance of the stifling "will of god". Stoker's *Dracula* has won that immortality, Coppola's "Dracula" will not.

HERETICS & MADMEN
THE WRITINGS OF THOMAS SZASZ

In 1960 CE Dr. Thomas Szasz issued a declaration of war against the psychiatric establishment. It came in the form of a book entitled, *The Myth Of Mental Illness.* As the title suggests, Dr. Szasz's contention is that mental illnesses are not real diseases, and that psychotherapy isn't real therapy, and that psychiatry isn't really science or medicine. Naturally enough, Dr. Szasz is regarded as a heretic by the aforementioned psychiatric establishment. This anathema has not deterred Dr. Szasz from continuing to point out the absurdities, contradictions and dangers of psychiatric dogma.

Ten years later, in *The Manufacture Of Madness* Dr. Szasz set forth a detailed argument that the inquisition had been replaced by the psychiatrists. It was always a popular theory that the heretics and witches of the middle ages were, in fact, lunatics. The common belief was that consigning these lunatics to the care of doctors was a huge step forward in the humane treatment of such people. It is well known that these early mad-houses were far from havens of humane treatment. Dr. Szasz goes into considerable detail on the tortures inflicted upon these "patients" in the name of enlightened medicine. One of the *"doctors"* discussed in this book is one of that illustrious company of culture gods, the Founding Fathers.

In 1978 CE *The Myth Of Psychotherapy* came out. In this book Dr. Szasz further discussed the religious nature of psychotherapy. This book discusses the nature of psychotherapy, as compared to legitimate therapies such as chemotherapy which act upon the body itself. Dr. Szasz does not say that psychotherapy is worthless, or that it should be done away with. Instead he suggests that it should be recognized as what it is, namely one person trying to convince another to change his mind, or his behavior. Rhetoric, not medicine. The book also looks at some of the figures involved in the evolution of psychotherapy, from Anton Mesmer to Freud

& Jung. Considerable space is devoted to looking at Freud's career.

One of the recurring themes in Dr. Szasz's books is the idea of the advent of what he calls the Therapeutic State. In the expansion of psychiatry into all aspects of life, and the growing belief that it is the duty of the state to guarantee the mental and physical health of its citizens, Dr. Szasz sees the specter of a totalitarian regime. A regime that incarcerates its heretics in psychiatric hospitals for the humanitarian purpose of restoring their sanity. What will constitute sanity? Acceptance of the gospel of psychiatry, conformity to social norms. In short, the herd is to be the standard of normalcy. We aren't likely to see a return of the old witch burnings. Don't concern yourself overmuch with the prospect of the Christians stacking up kindling for us. When they come for you it will probably be in an ambulance.

SAME OLD SONG & DANCE

During the recent media circus in Waco, Texas I was amused to read of the efforts of Christian clergy to distance themselves from the Branch Davidians. Now the Branch Davidians certainly do not represent the mainstream of Christian thought, but they are squarely within the tradition of the Judeo-Chrislamic religions. Judaism, Christianity and Islam all trace their origins to the same roots. The divergences from those roots came about because these religions are all highly prophet oriented—Moses, Isaiah, Jesus, Paul, Mohammed, Luther, Calvin the list goes on. Each of these men giving their own personal interpretation of the religion out of which they came. The history of these religions is a history of heresies opposing established orthodoxies. If a heresy lasts long enough it acquires legitimacy. Every Christian sect had its origin in a heresy. Today such heresies are almost invariably called "Cults" by the orthodox.

As I said, the history of these religions is one of persecution. Contrary to popular opinion this persecution rarely comes from without. Almost all persecution directed at any Judeo-Chrislamic sect comes from other such sects. With the proliferation of Christians in positions of authority it seems quite possible to me that the foolish and unnecessary attempt to lay siege to the Waco compound might have been devised by a highly placed Christian in the ATF as an attempt to discredit them. I can see no other reason for the fanatical zeal in the government handling of this affair. Anyone who doubts the influence of Christian ideas in U.S. policy decisions is encouraged to read Gregory Krupey's article "The Christian Right, Zionism, And The Coming Penteholocaust" in Feral House's *Apocalypse Culture.*

Considering how easily the government could've arrested David Koresh it seems quite apparent to me that the initial assault upon the Waco compound was probably motivated by the same Christian infighting that has been going on for centuries.

OBJECTIONS TO OBJECTIVISM

I have came across many references citing Ayn Rand as a Satanic writer. Granted, most of those who do this are Christian propagandists who cannot be taken seriously, but others who are more well disposed towards Satanism have done the same. While there are positive and useful things to be found in miss Rand's books I do not see how Objectivism, Ayn Rand's philosophy, can be equated with Satanism

Objectivism and Satanism differ in many ways. Objectivism approaches humanity with general good will; Satanism recognizes that humanity is generally unworthy of our good will. Objectivism buys into the freedom, and natural rights drivel contained in the Declaration of Independence; the Satanist knows that "natural" rights are not natural and that only the responsible few deserve freedom. The Objectivist sees man as something separate and apart from nature—a thinker, not a beast; the Satanist knows that man is a thinking beast bound up inextricably in the natural world. The Objectivist believes that time is strictly linear, progressing forward; the Satanist recognizes the "cycling of the ages of time". The Objectivist expresses belief in equality, despite Rand's recognition of the stratification inherent in nature; the Satanist dispenses with all such lip service to egalitarian notions.

I also have aesthetic differences with Rand, particularly in regard to architecture, which ordinarily I wouldn't give much consideration to, but since Rand is so dogmatic about it I will go into it. To Rand the pinnacle of architectural achievement is the skyscraper. All other forms of architecture are insignificant. The neoclassical style she is particularly contemptuous of. Admirers of these architectural styles are anathema to Rand. Personally, I find skyscrapers to be, for the most part, hideous. Not surprisingly Rand agrees with the popular assessment of so-called Totalitarian architecture. Had Hitler built tall glass and steel boxes she would sing a different tune, but since he preferred the gothic and neoclassical it is only natural that she rejects it. Like many others Rand argues that such monumentality is designed to make man feel small and insignificant. I don't see it that way myself. As I see it only the small and insignificant could be so intimidated by a building. Could it be that small and insignificant people cannot maintain their delusions of grandeur in the face of such true grandeur? It is easy for me to see how the masses could find inspiration in the sterile, monotonous uniformity of the modern skyscraper.

Despite their atheism the objectivists seem to adhere to the Christian concept that the earth exists for only one purpose—to provide raw materials for man's "progress". Considering its foundations in English enlightenment era philosophy it is hardly surprising that certain remnants of Christian thought, albeit rationalized Christian ideas, have been incorporated into Objectivist philosophy. The Objectivists agree with John Locke that land left in its natural state is land gone to waste. An Objectivist utopia would be a skyscraper-filled, coast to coast urban sprawl. Of course the mountains and forests would have to go, but think of the raw materials they'd yield up.

Rand would presume to take upon herself and her philosophy the mantle of Romanticism. I just don't see it. The Romantics and the Objectivists are worlds apart. The sense of tragedy and alienation so prevalent in the writings of the Romantics is entirely alien to Objectivism. The following quote from Peter Thorslev's book, *The Byronic Hero*, while referring to the poets and writers of the "enlightenment", can be applied to the Objectivists as well. "Dryden, Swift, Pope or Samuel Johnson were severe critics of the society in which they lived, to be sure, but they were always critics from within that society; they never at any time considered that they had some inner vision of truth not visible to the common readers of their age. They were quite convinced that all men could see as they did, if they but looked at nature in the light of their common reason and common sense." While there are analogies between Romanticism and Satanism, The Objectivists correspond more closely to these predecessors of the Romantics.

Rand, at times, went on about the Greeks as a model for western culture. What she meant by Greek culture was limited to classical sculpture and the philosophy of Aristotle; everything else must go. She accepts only the Apollonian aspects of Greek culture, rejecting out of hand the Dionysian elements of the culture. While she spoke approvingly of Greek art, she has no use for Greek drama since she saw tragedy as demeaning to man.

Central to Objectivism is the exaltation of reason and objectivity. It is because of this that Objectivism rejects categorically the Dionysian aspects of Greek culture. I find this pretense of objectivity to be one of the most annoying things about Objectivism. Certainly no one can deny that the world is full of objective facts. What is equally undeniable is that before these objective facts can be internalized by an individual they must be interpreted; raw data is ultimately useless. This interpretation is always subjective because it is based on individual experiences and biases. While subjectivity can be carried to extremes, to pretend at objectivity is no better.

Objectivism is, in the final analysis, an imbalanced, dualistic system. Like all such dualistic philosophies they reduce everything to simplistic black and white choices; in the world of the Objectivists there are no shades of gray. They would do well to learn the lesson Nietzsche taught in *The Birth Of Tragedy*—that it is the tension between the Apollonian and Dionysian drives that creates a vital society. Without this balance societies will drift towards either a morass of subjectivity and uncontrolled passions or a sterile, hyper-rational Apollonian nightmare. Unlike the Apollonian Objectivists the Satanist recognizes the necessity of this balance in nature.

MANFRED vs FAUST

I have no words, only a look for those who dare to say the word Faust in the presence of Manfred.
—Friedrich Nietzsche

With Byronic heroes "the mind is its own place"; each hero is, in a sense, beyond good and evil, he creates his own human values, and the sins of which he repents are transgressions of his own peculiar moral codes. For the commandments of religion or for common social morality he has nothing but defiance and contempt.
—Peter Thorslev

Some see in Goethe's *Faust* a Satanic archetype. I do not. Don't get me wrong, I am not saying that Goethe's version of the Faust legend is worthless. I am only saying that I don't see anything particularly Satanic in it. For one thing Faust's selling of his soul is un-Satanic, and for another the play is ultimately about redemption, as Faust is, in the end, carried off to heaven; hardly a Satanic aspiration.

I prefer *Manfred,* a play by Lord Byron. It forgoes the philosophical meanderings of Goethe's play and presents us with a figure of tragic heroism. Both plays open similarly, in the title character's study. Where Faust is just a jaded old man looking for a new experience to make his life meaningful, Manfred seeks forgetfulness. Though the specifics are not spelled out Manfred holds himself responsible for the death of his sister. This sense of guilt is not motivated by any Christian sensibilities though. Manfred has violated his own code of conduct and suffers because of it. One might be tempted to see this as self destructive, but it really isn't. What Manfred seeks is not self destruction, but rather self-overcoming. Where Faust comes across as a jaded dilettante, Manfred is a man who, though plunged into the depths of despair by his sense of responsibility and duty to himself, endures. A man who remains true to himself even if that means shouldering the responsibility for his own mistakes.

Manfred is not a soul seller. He commands the spirits in Satan's name and even goes to the court of Satan (called Arimanes in the play) and treats Satan as his equal. Right to the end, as both an evil spirit and a priest vie for his soul, Manfred steadfastly refuses to give up his soul to either side. In this Manfred is infinitely more Satanic than Faust.

Manfred also displays the telltale alienation that marks our kind as the following passage demonstrates. The speaker is Manfred. "From my youth upwards my spirit walked not with the souls of men, nor looked upon the earth with human eyes; the thirst of their ambition was not mine, the aim of their existence was not mine; my joys—my griefs my passions—and my powers made me a stranger; though I wore the form I had no sympathy with breathing flesh... with men, and with the thoughts of men I held but slight communion... for if the beings, of whom I was one—hating to be so—crossed me in my path I felt degraded back to them."

Some have said that *Manfred* was just a Byronic take on Goethe's story but I don't buy it. In all probability Byron was inspired by the Faust legend but the similarities between *Manfred* and *Faust* can also be found in Marlowe's *Tragedy Of Dr. Faustus.* No, *Manfred* is not just a copy of *Faust.* It may begin with certain parallels but they do not represent the same ideas.

TRADITIONAL SATANISM?

Of late I've been hearing a lot about "traditional Satanism". What is "traditional Satanism"? That depends on who is doing the talking. Everything from Gnosticism to Eliphas Levi, Freemasonry to Thelema has been put forth as an example of "traditional Satanism" If you want to talk to the Christians they'll tell you that it consists of the ritual mutilation, torture and sacrifice of everything from chickens to children. Conspicuously, all of those who try to sell "traditional Satanism" attempt to place their origins before the birth of the Church of Satan.

If these "traditional Satanists" existed before that time where were they? They didn't exist, or else they weren't calling themselves "Satanists". Before the advent of the Church of Satan nobody would touch the name of Satanism with a ten foot pole. Back then "Satanist" was what you called your enemies, not yourself. Even if we give these people the benefit of the doubt, which I don't, and accept their claims of antiquity we must ask why they rejected the name of Satanism. To my mind such cowardice would automatically deny them any claim to the name. Now I am certainly not in favor of martyrdom, it would have been possible for these various "Traditional Satanists" to come out in the open before 1966 CE. These people are, for the most part, a mixed bag of left handed Thelemites, Freemasons, and quasi-Christian pseudo-Satanists. I can understand why they want to cash in on the name of Satanism, but I do not accept their claims.

Satanism is a very eclectic system. We borrow whatever we like from a broad range of sources. We take what we will from other traditions and turn it to our purposes. We are not obligated to adhere to the traditions of those from whom we have borrowed. The Christians complain about how Satanists have twisted Satan into something that he is not. They do not understand that we aren't obliged to interpret their myths, their way. We borrowed their devil, and made of him something better, something our own. In the same way the adherents of hermetic magic might complain that Satanism takes some of their ideas about ritual magic and wrenches them out of context. That would be fine if we were hermetic magicians, but we are not. We are Satanists, and we have established our own tradition. We expect no one else to abide by our traditions unless they choose to wear our name.

I am not attacking these so-called "traditional Satanists" because of what they are. There are points of disagreement between their assorted ideas and ours, but there is agreement as well. I have no objection to their existence, but I do object to their misappropriation of the name of Satanism. They are what they are, they should wear their own names, not ours. The various and sundry schools of "traditional Satanic" thought may parallel Satanic thought to some degree or another, but in the final analysis they aren't Satanism. The Church of Satan is Satanism, "traditional Satanism" is not.

HEAVEN & HELL

The mind is its own place, and in itself can make a Heav'n of Hell, a Hell of Heav'n... Better to reign in Hell than serve in Heav'n.

—John Milton

The Satanist, much to the consternation of the Christians, doesn't believe in a literal Hell, God's torture chamber, a place of fire and endless torment, but then we don't believe in Satan either. Since we make use of Satan we might as well use Hell also.

As I see it, Heaven and Hell are states of mind. Satanists have a Hellish mind set, while Christians and their ilk have a heavenly mind set. The differences between these states of mind are fundamental. This explains why the multitudes of Heavenly minded drones find us so incomprehensible.

The quote above, from *Paradise Lost* perfectly sums up the essential nature of both of these mind sets. One, Heaven, is oriented towards servitude; the other to sovereignty.

In "Heaven", the Christian mind set, the individual will is forfeited. The heavenly exist to serve the "will of god". This is not necessarily the will of god as the Christians would understand it. For example, a teenager who decides to realize the fanciful imaginings of the talk show pseudo-Satanists and do "Satan's will", or a person who decides that it is his obligation to selflessly serve the homeless, the hungry or any other parasitic group, are of a heavenly mind set whether they recognize it or not. Any attitude of "not my will but thine be done", or "what I want is unimportant" is evidence of a heavenly mentality.

On the other hand, Hell is a mentality dedicated to the fulfillment of the personal will. To submit without question is alien to the hellish mind. The hellishly minded follow the dictates of their own will, their own desires. They do not want to be relieved of responsibility at the cost of their freedom. The hellish individual realizes that though he may not be a king, he is not a slave and serves no master, or god, but himself. The heavenly minded will throw away their own sovereignty for the illusion of redemption. The hellish know that there is no need for it.

The rise of democracy indicated a crumbling of the heavenly mind set. The sheep want freedom; unfortunately they want to keep their shepherd as well. Freedom and irresponsibility are incompatible. If you want to be your own master you must first dispense with other masters. Modern democracy is a feeble attempt to bridge the gap between Heaven and Hell. It won't work. The two realms are too fundamentally different. There can be no freedom for the heavenly. It is their lot to serve.

Freedom is the prerogative of Hell.

THOUGHTS ON FREE WILL

Does free will exist? Yes, but practically speaking it has its limitations. The degree of free will a person can exercise will be limited by their past experiences, and their instinctual impulses. Some degree of choice exists along this natural, instinctually ordered course, but it certainly doesn't include the full spectrum of options from A to Z. You are, of course, free to deviate from the course ordained by instinct, but this will prove ultimately unsatisfying. Jose Ortega y Gasset said "every living creature is happy when he fulfills his destiny, that is, when he realizes himself, when he is being that which in truth he is", and this is quite true. While we are free to try and be other than what we truly are, and are meant to be, it is not a wise thing to do. The further we stray from this instinctual path the more lost we will become. To follow the course laid by another persons instincts will only take you where they are meant to be. You may not belong there.

In *Thus Spake Zarathustra* Nietzsche puts these words in Zarathustra's mouth: "I need living companions who follow me because they want to follow themselves—and who want to go where I want to go." If you are following someone, anyone, who is not going to where your instincts are telling you to go then you are on a dead end course. It is only in this sense that you should follow another. To use a more mundane metaphor, if you needed to go somewhere you could follow anyone in the hope of getting there, but if they aren't going there you could get lost and have to spend a great deal of time and effort in getting back on track. You are free to follow anyone, but if they aren't going your way why would you want to?

Many people in the modern world are not following their instincts. This is a society that denies the very existence of instinct in humans. Instinctive drives are dismissed as irrationality; as mere whims. People have buried their instinctive selves so deeply that they no longer hear its voice outside of dreams, where it often is ignored or misunderstood. Some will, in time, escape this trap, but countless others will go on, locked in a rut of emptiness and dissatisfaction without even understanding why this is.

Many people turn away from their instincts because, on the surface, the dictates of instinct might seem irrational. Irrational according to whom? Who is it that has dictated the standards by which you live? We are animals, all of us, and as such we are born with an innate awareness of who and what we are. Do not allow others to divert you from your true path. Modern society wants standardized components for the machine, and if your instincts would deter you from such a course then society will try to warp and twist you in such a way as to make you a useful cog in the social mechanism. They might tell you that these rules are for your benefit but it's a lie. If your instincts tell you to be something other than a part in the machine, listen to them.

SACRED?

It has been said that there is a sanctity in human life; that human life, as such, is always of immeasurable value. Some animal rights advocates go so far as to say that ALL life is sacred. They obviously don't really believe this since plants, insects, bacteria and viruses, life forms all, are exempt from sacred status. Sometimes people will speak of this modern regard for the "sacredness of human life" as an advance from the barbaric attitudes of the past. If this is so then I must confess to being a barbarian.

I do not believe that life is sacred. Life, as these people define it is a mere biological function. In their eyes so long as you are not dead your life retains the same value it always has. Some of the more extreme sorts stretch this period of static and innate value back to the moment of conception. To suggest that everyone who is not dead has the same intrinsic value is ludicrous, and yet even supposedly intelligent people have endorsed this belief.

In part this arises from most people's need for simple, black and white choices. Since death is undesirable at some time or another in life then it must be undesirable at all times. To suggest that life is not invariably good, nor death invariably bad, is entirely unacceptable. It forces a value judgment. It introduces a shade of gray into an otherwise stark black and white landscape.

The recent efforts on the part of the government of the United States to create a universal health care system have stirred the wrath of many people because the question has been asked, when do you "pull the plug". The masses, with their blind fear and loathing of death, would have their wretched lives prolonged indefinitely at public expense if possible. As if they are worth such efforts.

The health care system is a strong supporter of this life at any price philosophy. I came across the following statements in a newspaper interview with a local doctor. "Other nations let people die when they could live. If a baby is under two pounds in Sweden, they let it die. Here we would... see it gets maximum care. If a baby gets heroic measures, a large amount of money is spent—about $500,000 to get it to the first grade." The doctor lets the cat out of the bag in that last sentence. The medical establishment doesn't really believe in the sanctity of human life, but they do know that dead men pay no bills. For that reason they are quite happy to fill the world with vast hordes of weak, sickly, wretched examples of human garbage to fatten their bank accounts. The doctor bemoans the fact that terminal patients are denied treatment in some countries. Why terminal patients should be treated, when such treatments are admittedly futile, is not addressed by the good doctor, but the only good reason for it is so that he can be paid. This also explains the persecution of Dr. Kevorkian. It simply won't do for hopelessly sick people to decide that death is better. They must not "give up". They must hang on to life, and above all they must keep going to see the doctor.

Over a century ago Friedrich Nietzsche wrote, in *Twilight of the Idols,* "The invalid is a parasite on society. In a certain state it is indecent to go on living. To vegetate on in cowardly dependence on physicians and medicaments after the meaning of life, the right to life, has been lost ought to entail the profound contempt of society. Physicians, in their turn, ought to be the communicators of this contempt—not prescriptions, but every day a fresh dose of disgust with their patients... To create a new responsibility, that of the physician, in all cases in which the highest interest of life, of ascending life, demands the most ruthless suppression and sequestration of degenerating life." We need such a state of affairs even more today because society has had another century to slip into further decay. It was shameful that Nietzsche's sister made a mockery of her brother's work by displaying his decrepit husk years after he should've died. It is doubly shameful that such husks are still with us after all these years.

I am not in love with death. For death to befall the vigorous, useful individual before his or her time is indeed tragic. But death is a part of life. Hiding from it, or denying it is futile for it will come to all of us. Death is, in itself, neither good or bad. It can tragically cut short promising lives, or it can clear away the old and sick so that the health of the species can be improved. As Robert Ardrey has said, "if life is to be regarded as essentially good then death must be seen as its foremost angel". Death and life are inextricably bound together. In the proper balance there is no discord between them.

NIHILISM

Many people consider Satanism to be a nihilistic philosophy. They do this because they are ignorant. They are either ignorant of what Satanism really is, or they are ignorant of what nihilism is, or perhaps they are truly benighted and are ignorant of both. It should be no surprise therefore that Christianity has been at the forefront of such accusers since Christianity and ignorance are virtually synonymous. Those ignorant of Satanism usually are of the belief that Satanists are interested only in destruction. They believe that we have in some sense deified the principle of destructiveness. Those ignorant of the definition of nihilism will generally define it as a belief in nothing. This is not the definition of nihilism. It is true that Satanism is not characterized by belief, or faith in groundless ideas like gods, or absolute moral laws, but that is not nihilism. The definition of nihilism is more accurately stated as "The will to nothingness". The nihilist wants to see all that is pass away with nothing to replace it. Nihilism is destruction with no constructive element. The nihilist does not destroy to clear the ground for new development, they just destroy. The nihilist is for nothing. The nihilist is that which is against what is. He is the enemy of existence.

The examples which allegedly prove the nihilism of Satanism are, by and large, examples of not Satanism, but Devil worship. This motley assortment of scum and vermin are not Satanists by any stretch of the imagination. They are what many have accused us of being, mere parasites clinging to the body of Christianity. They are merely Antichrists, the bastards of Christianity. There is no positive element to their philosophy, if you can grace their muddle of ideas with that term. It is only negative. While the Satanist *too* is an Antichrist, he is not *just* an Antichrist. The Satanist has a vision of a Satanic world, not just of the destruction of the Christian world. A desire to not just destroy Christianity but to go beyond it.

As I noted earlier, Christians most often bring these charges of nihilism against us. In actuality it is the Christian who follows a nihilistic philosophy. As Nietzsche stated in *The Antichrist* "Life is denied, made more worthy of denial by pity—pity is practical nihilism... pity persuades to nothingness!... One does not say 'nothingness': one says 'the beyond'; or 'God'; or 'true life'; or Nirvana, redemption, blessedness... This innocent rhetoric from the domain of religio-moral idiosyncrasy at once appears much less innocent when one grasps which tendency is here draping the mantle of sublime words about itself: the tendency hostile to life." Christianity, with its fanatical love of the life to come is rife with nihilism. They want to see the world perish. "There now, by your own definition we cannot be nihilists for we too have a vision of something better" say the Christians. They think that their Heaven will suffice to nullify any accusations of nihilism against them. It won't. We understand that the "Will to Heaven" is in fact the "Will to Nothing" for the Christian's Heaven *IS nothing!*

PAGANISM & THE DEIFICATION OF CULTURE

Once I was sent a "Satanic" publication which contained this statement—"I will no longer sit back and tolorate(*sic)* unjust and brutal attacks against our Pagan beliefs!!". While I grant that this was a pretty wretched publication it does illustrate this point. I believe that there is a move afoot by some in the "Satanic" community to identify Satanism with Paganism. This is an error.

I am not suggesting that alliances are impossible. I am saying that it is a mistake to believe that "the enemy of my enemy is my friend". That is the credo of a fool. The enemy of my enemy is just that. Aside from a common foe we may have nothing else in common and in fact may well turn out to be enemies. The Allied forces of World War II illustrate this point very well. In the case of the various Paganisms which are sometimes looked upon as friendly to Satanism I believe that this may ultimately prove to be true.

There are some parallels between Satanism and the various Pagan systems. This is not surprising. Satanism is quite open about its syncretistic ways. We borrowed the best from the many strains of Pagan thought just as Christianity borrowed the worst. Even the similarities vanish upon closer examination. As an example let's take Odinism. Superficially one might think that there are certain affinities between the ethical stance of Odinism and that of Satanism but when you consider the motivations you see that the similarities are, just as I said, superficial. A Satanist is a Satanist because he has Satanic values. A Pagan has Pagan values because he's a Pagan. Furthermore, he is probably a Pagan because it is his "heritage".

Earlier I discussed the heavenly and hellish mindsets. These two ways of looking at the world can be summarized briefly as "thy will be done", the heavenly mindset, as opposed to "my will be done", which is the hellish view. Satanism promotes the hellish view but Paganism, with its deification of "tradition" and "cultural heritage" is decidedly heavenly in its outlook. I find this attitude very silly, yet it is a part of virtually all Pagan beliefs. In memory of the Hitlerian Germanic culture cult I will call this attitude Volkishness.

The volkish argument goes like this: Only Jews should be Christian because Christianity is a sub-sect of Judaism. Since non-Jews were Pagans two thousand years ago they should still be pagan. I've heard it expressed in the statement "We weren't meant to be Christians". This is, in a word, stupid. On the one hand it implies that there is some kind of cosmic plan and everything is "meant to be". There is no such "meaning" in events. On the other hand it assumes that the Pagan beliefs of past centuries would've remained unchanging through the centuries. Who's to say that any Pagan system would've survived to the present even without Christianity? Furthermore it assumes that the Paganisms of two thousand years ago always were. Consider the Norse myths. There is every reason to believe that at one time the Jotuns, or giants, were worshipped and that they were supplanted by the worship of the Aesir, the classic Norse gods, who then followed the time honored practice of turning the old gods into devils. Shouldn't the Odinists therefore worship the Jotuns instead since their ancestors probably worshipped them before they worshipped Odin and company? How far back are we to go?

The devotees of "the goddess" say that the worship of mother goddesses preceeded most other paganisms since such beliefs go back to neolithic times, but why stop there? During the ice ages a bear cult flourished in Europe. Should everyone of European descent worship bears? This can get pretty silly. According to the volkish argument I should not be a Satanist since Satanism has Jewish elements in it and I have no Jewish ancestors. There is a problem though. My ancestry is a blend of Germanic and Celtic with a little bit of American Indian. Does this mean that I should worship the Aesir one day and the Tuatha De Danann the next with a prayer to some indian "great spirit" thrown in every couple of weeks? As you can clearly see, this is ridiculous. Pagans would object that I should choose one, but how could I do that? If I am free to choose to reject part of my "heritage", why should I be obligated to any of it?

The principal thrust of all Pagan arguments fall back upon this idea of following ones cultural heritage, but why should I place limitations on myself based upon some dead culture? The volkish attitude treats culture as something delivered full blown in the dawn of time. A gift of the gods as it were. All living cultures borrow from other sources. Satanism is a culture unto itself. It is a living, growing culture. Proponents of volkishness might consider this attitude as an act of treason against "my people". I laugh at such idiocies. What is it to me where my ancestors lived? They are dead. As it says in Robert E. Howard's excellent poem *EMPIRE: A Song For All Exiles* "Heritage of the world is ours", every culture that has ever existed is a part of that heritage. The world lies before me. I will take what I will and cast aside what I will and cultural purity be damned. It is one thing to look back and see something admirable and say to yourself that this or that is a thing worthy of bringing forth and incorporating into your culture, but to embrace what has been and say that this is what was meant to be is to seal yourself into a tomb locked in an embrace with a corpse.

Ultimately Paganism has far more in common with Christianity than with Satanism, just listen to a Pagan talking about his "spirituality" and you'll understand this. Like Christians the Pagans believe grovelling in the dust before a god to be a virtue. There is a line in an old Mercyful Fate song that states the Satanic view clearly and concisely. That line is, "I don't need your god!". That doesn't just mean I don't need Yahweh & son. It means that I don't need *any* god! While they might be enemies of Christianity they are no friends of ours. To consider them to be our friends is short sighted and foolish.

The gods are dead! Let us dance on their graves.

ENTERING THE ABYSS: THE PSYCHOLOGY OF MAGIC

The following essay touches upon ritual and magic. Some of the ideas in this article were inspired and influenced by the ideas of C.G. Jung but they are not, properly speaking, Jungian. In my opinion, while there is much in Jung's work that is admirable he was still far too Christian in his outlook. I do not claim that these ideas constitute any sort of revealed word. It works for me. If you don't like it feel free to stick with your own ideas and interpretations.

The Powers That Be

To the Satanist, Satan and the other devils are not real entities. They are however what might be termed "psychic entities". I do not mean to imply anything metaphysical or paranormal in using the word *psychic.* I refer simply to the mind. The only existence Satan and the other devils have is in the mind. They are the personifications of impersonal forces of nature, or of the dark, instinctive drives of mankind. Asmodeus is called a demon of lust. What does this mean? It means that man has given the energy which drives his lust a name. To invoke Asmodeus is not to call forth a spirit out of Hell; rather it is to call forth that lustful energy. All of the devils listed in *The Satanic Bible* under the heading of The Infernal Names are such archetypal forces. They reside in the deepest levels of the psyche. The unconscious mind, both personal and collective. This unconscious mind I call the Abyss.

The Abyss

The Abyss from which these devils are summoned is the unconscious mind. The unconscious mind is not the same thing as the subconscious mind, which is a sort of junk doset of the mind. The unconscious mind is the realm of dreams. The language of the unconscious is the language of symbolism. The unconscious mind cares nothing for the rationality and logic of ordinary, conscious reality.

The unconscious mind is very old. Because many of the symbolic motifs of the unconscious are the same the world over the unconscious mind probably evolved to something much like its present state before the differentiation of the races. The mental differences between differing racial groups tend to be differences on the conscious levels.

Most people enter into this unconscious realm only in their dreams. Even then they find this part of their minds inexplicable because they try and apply to this dark domain the rules which govern conscious thought. In the ritual chamber the Satanist tries to consciously alter into this unconscious mind. The directional symbolism tells you as much. The east and west are governed by Lucifer and Leviathan respectively. Lucifer represents enlightenment. Leviathan is the serpent out of the deep. These are metaphors for the well lit realm of consciousness and the murky depths of the unconscious. In facing west one turns ones back on the conscious mind so as to enter into the realm of the archetypes, the unconscious mind-the Abyss.

The Four Princes

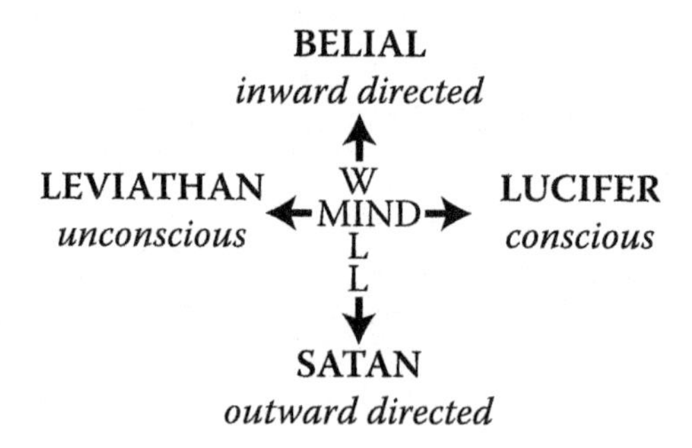

In *The Satanic Bible* Anton LaVey speaks of the four Crown Princes of Hell. These are Satan, Lucifer, Belial and Leviathan. He lists a directional and elemental correspondence for each. I also see a psychological correspondence. As I see it the north-south axis represents what Nietzche called the Will To Power. This Will To Power is exerted in two ways. On the north end of this axis we have Belial, who is without a master. Belial represents the Will To Power turned inward so as to attain self-mastery. In this sense Belial corresponds to the Apollonian drive. At the other end we have Satan, the adversary, who goes forth to dominate and exercise this Will To Power upon the world around him. Accordingly Satan can be seen as being somewhat Dionysian. The Apollo/Dionysus analogy is limited and should not be carried to too great an extreme. The Apollonian side would more accurately encompass both Belial and Lucifer, correspondingly the Dionysian would encompass Satan and Leviathan. The east-west axis represents mind. As I have already stated, the east represents the conscious, Luciferian mind. The west end is the unconscious, Leviathanic mind. The diagram I have provided graphically shows this. As you can see, at the center is I. This represents the individual.

The Satanist should strive for balance and center himself along both axes. He may not always do so but it should be the goal toward which he strives.

Magic

Synchronicity is a name Jung gave to meaningful co-incidence. As I see it, magic is an attempt to induce such synchronistic events. Jung spoke of three types of synchronicity. Two correspond to what is now known as psychic phenomena and do not concern us here. The remaining type is defined by Jean Bolen, a Jungian analyst, in her book *The Tao of Psychology* in this way. "A coincidence between mental content (which could be a thought or feeling) and outer event."

Synchronistic events are most common when powerful emotions are combined with unconscious mental activity. Therefore, synchronicity most often occurs without any conscious awareness of it. In ritual one enters into the Abyss and through strong emotions attempts to trigger such synchronistic events.

It is not only Synchronicity that the witch or warlock seeks to manipulate through ritual. By operating in the Abyss of the unconscious you enter into that vast web which binds us all: the collective unconscious. You might think of it as a vast phone network. You can call anyone if you have their number. A powerful emotional connection, be it love, hate or something in between, establishes that link. The means by which you then communicate is a sort of telepathic communication. This is not to be understood in the science fiction sense of having a mind to mind conversation. No, I'm referring to something born of the unconscious and which might never enter into the consciousness of the recipient, but then it doesn't need to. I am referring to the sending of impressions or gut-feelings which are intended to influence people in ways desirable to the magician. To give an example, you might send out very powerful emotions to sow fear in the heart of your adversary, or lust in the mind of one you desire. They need not be aware of these thoughts consciously, and in many cases it is best if they do not.

Some might suggest that the prayer of the Christians constitutes a form of magic. Perhaps you might look upon it as a sort of bastardized, guilt-ridden magic at best. The Satanist speaks of the IS-TO-BE while the Christian speaks halfheartedly of the IF-IT-BE-THY-WILL-OH-LORD. From time to time they might have an emotion strong enough to cut through this pious bullshit, and if so I might be able to consider it a form of magic, otherwise if a prayer comes true it is either chance or possibly a case of simple synchronicity. Magic is an act of will, and the results must be willed, not begged for like a cringing, grovelling slave.

SMELLS LIKE A DEAD JUNKIE

There's a new god in Rock Heaven. Kurt Cobain, of the band Nirvana, a sorry little maggot who pissed and moaned about his fame all the way to the bank, took the royal road to rock divinity—self destruction.

This two-bit heroin addict would've probably been forgotten in a few years time; but now since he opted to end the life he so often bitched about he is acclaimed as a major talent, the "voice of a generation" and other such bullshit. I saw a picture of this wretch on the cover of *Newsweek* magazine with a caption asking why people killed themselves. In Cobain's case this is a pretty simple question to answer. He was too damned weak to survive. The fact that he was a heroin addict tells you that. Would that all such weaklings would do themselves in, and in so doing do the world an inestimable favor.

I was told that in the wake of Cobain's apotheosis, MTV started running spots telling young Nirvana fans not to commit suicide in imitation of their idol. While I can understand MTV's economic motivations for such an action it would've been much better for the species had they instead run spots telling anyone weak minded enough to kill themselves just because some strung out singer did so to go ahead and do it. Maybe running specific instructions so the little bastards would get it right. It would've been nice to hear of a rash of copycat suicides following Cobain's.

Many in the media called Cobain's death a tragedy. The only tragedy I see is that he and his wife, another heroin addict, managed to spawn a child before his demise. I suppose it is possible that the child will ultimately rise above the level of its parents, but I wouldn't bet on it. When you come right down to it this is just another death of a worthless human being. It's not a mystery and certainly not a tragedy. It's more like a drop in the bucket. After all, what's one more dead junkie in the grand scheme of things?

LEGITIMIZING LOVECRAFT

H.P. Lovecraft's "Cthulhu Mythos" is apparently quite popular these days amongst Satanists. This is easy to understand. Lovecraft's godless cosmology is one that the Satanist can easily relate to. However, it does seem odd to me that many Satanists who draw inspiration from Lovecraft have turned to the various attempts to "legitimize" Lovecraft through books which purport to be the *real Necronomicon.*

The first I'll mention is the *Necronomicon* published by Skoob books. This one is a rather shoddy effort to place Lovecraft's Mythos within the framework of Elizabethan magic. Basically what they did was to slip a few Lovecraftian names, or bits of terminology, into an old grimoire. Oddly enough, despite the book's ridiculous claim to being the "real" *Necronomicon,* the various "quotations" from the *Necronomicon* cited by Lovecraft in his stories do not appear in this book.

Far more popular is the notorious Necronomicon of Simon. This version attempts to give Lovecraft's Great Old Ones legitimacy by trying to create spurious connections between Lovecraft's Cthulhu Mythos and the Mythology of the ancient Sumerians. This *Necronomicon* is also lacking those passages cited by Lovecraft in his own works. It really seems odd to me that this one has lasted as long as it has since even a cursory examination of the Sumerian mythology will reveal that Azag-Thoth, Shub Ishniggurab, and Kutulu were not gods in the Sumerian pantheon, nor were they referred to in the Sumerian religious texts.

One thing that both of these ersatz *Necronomicons* have in common is their agreement with the absurd ideas of August Derleth. This is probably because Derleth's childishly dualistic conception meshes better with their Sumerian and Elizabethan contexts.

I can readily understand why believers of conventional occultism would want to try to legitimize Lovecraft's make believe mythology by connecting it to some "real" mythology, or system of magic. What is more difficult for me to understand is why

Satanists would do so. The Satanist should be used to thinking of all religions and systems as just make believe. If you are magically inspired by the imagery of Lovecraft's stories then Cthulhu is as real as he needs to be. He is every bit as real as Marduk, Ishtar, Satan, or any other mythological figure. The only difference is that Lovecraft admitted that he created Cthulhu. If you are magically inspired by Lovecraft's stories, why not use the stories themselves as a source instead of some phony *pseudo-Necronomicon*?

ROBERT E. HOWARD: SATANIC SKALD

Some of you may know who Robert E. Howard was. To many he was just the creator of Conan the Cimmerian. Others may know that Howard was a correspondent of H.P. Lovecraft, and wrote some stories belonging to the "Cthulhu mythos", in fact, Howard created one of the many tomes of forbidden lore that is mentioned in the stories, the *Unaussprechlichen Kulten*, or Nameless Cults, of Von Juntz. There is however another aspect of Howard's writing which has often been sadly neglected. I am referring to his poetry.

Howard's poetic works are often difficult to find. I am not aware of any volume which collected all of his poems in one place.* They are often relegated to being filler. They deserve better than that. Howard's poetic muse was often a very dark one, and a violent one as well. I cannot print Howard's poems in their entirety owing to copyright laws, but I will quote from some in an effort to introduce you to these wonderful poems.

True rime concerns her not with bursting buds,
The chirping bird, the lifting of the rose—
Save ebon blooms that swell in ghastly woods,
And that grim, voiceless bird that ever broods
Where through black boughs a wind of horror blows.
—"Which Will Scarcely Be Understood"

As Howard himself put it, "The little poets sing of little things" among these little things are numbered, hope, cheer, faith, "lovers who kissed and were made as one" and flowers. Howard's poems are about the pinnacles of joy and the depths of despair. Of drinking from the cup of life to its fullest, and the emptiness which is the

---

* *Editor's note*—There have been a few small press collections of R.E. Howard's poetry published. Since the time of this essay's writing there has been a now out-of-print volume collecting over 700 examples, and claiming to be complete.

ultimate destiny of that cup of life. The voices Howard assumes in his poems are the voices of men who know that life is meaningless, that all that really exists is the here and now. The poetry of Robert E. Howard is akin to that of the berserker poets of old.

He writes of the war of the true, fully human, man, the man who is at one with the beast within, against the domesticated, overly civilized man and the priests who has made him what he is. One of my favorite poems is "EMPIRE: A Song For All Exiles". In it Howard speaks for "we who ride for the one Black Master",and says "We have plunged our hands in the wine of the Devil, leave the saints to their paradise". In one of my favorite passages he says, "Praised be the prince that reigns forever, Throned in the shadows stark and grim, Where cypress moans by the midnight river—Lift your goblets and drink to him!"

> You say God's spark, has kindled my eye,
> As the sun-rise reddens the east;
> Into your beards I roar the lie–
> Tis the gleam of the Stalking beast.
>
> –"The Dust Dance"

> "Fool, fool, you came unbidden to this game,
> And death that takes you hence shall ask you not.
> From life, this and only this, may you claim;
> Living, to die, and dying, be forgot."
>
> –"A Sonnet Of Good Cheer"

On June 11th, 1936, Howard, after so often talking about and contemplating suicide, shot himself through the head. It is indeed paradoxical that often great art is born of such flaws. It is perhaps the mark of the true artist that they can turn such weakness into strength, for a while at least. This truism all too often leads to the mistaken idea that every third rate hack who does himself in, whether through a quick suicide or something slower like booze or drugs, is a great artist. In Howard's case however I believe that such a statement fits. We must be careful though to understand that while this inner weakness led to his death, it also led to his art. For this reason the "tragedy" of the death of the artist is somewhat mitigated. It is the necessary final act. Nothing else will suffice. When the hack dies he is just getting out of the way, when the artist dies he has completed his work and has put the finishing touch upon his life. While this view might seem cold to some I feel that it is the only viable one on the matter. I do not weep for Howard, I rejoice in the poems he left us, poetry which stokes the black flame within.

> Ring up the demons from the lower Pit,
> Since Evil conquers goodness in the end;
> Break down the Door and let the fires be lit.
> And greet each slavering monster as a friend.
> Let obscene shapes of Darkness ride the earth,
> Let sacrificial smokes blot out the skies,
> Let dying virgins glut the Black God's eyes,
> And all the world resound with noisome mirth.
> Break down the altars, let the streets run red.
> Tramp down the race into the crawling slime;
> Then where red Chaos lifts her serpent head,
> The fiend be praised we'll pen the perfect rime.
>
> —"Which Will Scarcely Be Understood"

Robert E. Howard understood the Satanic spirit. The effort to search out some of his poetry will pay a handsome dividend in inspiration. They are truly gems.

> Thunder from the grim gulfs,
> out of the cosmic deep,
> Where the red eyes glimmer
> and the black wings sweep,
> Thunder down to Satan,
> wake him from his sleep!
>
> —"Red Thunder"

THE ENEMY

I have noticed a tendency on the part of some Satanists to dwell upon, if you will excuse the expression, the evils of Christianity. Now Christianity is certainly a contemptible religion, and it has had a truly detrimental effect upon mankind throughout its history but it should not be seen as *THE* enemy. The Christian religion is dying out. Most of those who call themselves Christians do so more out of conventionality than anything else. It is socially acceptable so they keep the tag. If there were a social stigma attached to being a Christian they would shed the label in a minute. No, the weed of Christianity is withering fast but the soil in which it grew remains.

I do not mean to suggest that Christianity is no longer a problem. Christians still retain a pretty high nuisance value. In fact, now that the realization that Christianity, as such, is dying has set in, the fanatical fringe is growing more active. While this is a potentially dangerous situation, after all, some Christian "holy warrior" might decide to target the "Devil's servant"—*you*—for termination, ultimately it will be their downfall as it will help to create that aforementioned social stigma.

Even if Christianity were to die tomorrow and the name of Christ be forgotten our true enemy would remain. That enemy is the decadence and weakness which embraced Christianity two thousand years ago. Just because it no longer needs religion to spread its message do not think it is dead. What we have today is a situation where the chandala ethic which found voice in Christian religion has been internalized to such an extent that these values have become second nature to most people. Those who do not accept these values at once become the target of an exhaustive effort to either warp them to fit the expected norms or demoralize them into an ineffectual state. These slave culture values, values such as democracy, egalitarianism are the real enemy. Where Satanism endorses personal responsibility and strength the chandala values are characterized by a sense of pervasive victimization and weakness.

Weakness that allows compassion for the unfit is the enemy. Weakness that says that forgiveness is a virtue is the enemy. Weakness that says that everybody is equal is the enemy. Weakness that says that the group is more important than the individual is the enemy. Weakness that looks to spiritualism rather than materialism for truth is the enemy. The real enemy shall always exist, and ultimately that is as it should be (see the Book Of Satan V:10), but after our victory is completed we must keep it in its place. A slave must have slave values but a world that glorifies slave values is an abomination.

Christianity is, for all intents and purposes, dead. It might be fun to kick the corpse but it isn't very useful. Instead, turn your attention to the real enemy.

KILLING TIME: *Thoughts on Dealing with Christians and Kindred Vermin*

I occasionally get letters from people asking me how best to deal with Christians—although from time to time other groups will be named, most similar to Christians in some sense or other. Perhaps the best answer is to deal with them as briefly, and as infrequently, as possible. However, this answer is seldom considered satisfactory by these inquirers. What follows are a few thoughts on the subject.

Some people want to know: "How can you convince these people that they are wrong and you are right?" My first thought is, "Who cares?" Such debates generally go nowhere. Now, if this is something that you feel is really important, all you can do is set your facts and evidences forth. If your audience is like most Christians, you will accomplish little or, more likely, nothing by doing so. To a Christian, the only "facts" that matter are found between the covers of a Bible. You cannot reason with people who believe that their God has exalted the foolish and chooses to work through miracles. Ask yourself this question: "Why am I so concerned with what this idiot thinks of me?"

Others ask how best to win Christians over to our side. I normally respond to such a question with one of my own: "Who wants them?" Let's pretend for a moment that you were actually able to convince this Christian half-wit that Satanism is the way to go—what then? I'll tell you what. It won't be long before the misguided fool will be looking, for a cat, goat, or baby to sacrifice to Satan—his "personal savior" who has now replaced Jesus. Why? Because he won't accept our definition of Satanism; he'll look to what his former Christian brethren define as Satanism. These people can't understand Satanism, are plainly unsuited to a Satanic philosophy of life, and introducing them to one isn't going to make things better for anybody. There are few things worse than a Christian who decides to devote himself to "sin and wickedness." They will become pointlessly destructive and will wind up making a horrible mess of everything with which they come in contact. You think that they are a nuisance as Christians? Try and "convert" them all to "Satanism," then you'll find out what assholes they can be when they really try. As Christians, they are usually feeble and ineffectual enough. It's best to let sleeping lambs lie, but persistently annoying lambs can make good "lamb chops." More on that later.

Some of my inquirers want to know how they can convince Christians that we are really nice people. Answer: You can't. If you are a Satanist, then by Christian standards, you are not a nice person. The mere fact that you choose to identify with what they perceive as the source of "Ultimate Evil" tells them that you are not nice. Learn to live with it. Again, why do you care about what they think of you? Are they people you know well? If so, they ought to be able to decide from direct experience whether you are a nice guy. If they would think that you are nice enough, except for that awful name you stick on yourself, then they are obviously not worth your time. Let's face facts here. You are not going to be popular with Christians if you call yourself a Satanist. Why would anyone think otherwise?

What many of these questioners fail to take into account is that it isn't just a question of freedom of choice. Truly committed Christians, and I'm not talking about nominal Christians or social Christians here, cannot be other than what they are. You've all heard the old saw about describing red to a person with color blindness—it can't be done. It's the same with trying to gain acceptance from a true Christian. Nominal and social Christians can be won over to some degree, because their dedication to Christianity (and thus commitment to hating its "enemies") is far more tenuous, being born out of laziness, habit, or social convention. But I can't really see why anybody would want to devote the time and energy needed to accomplish such a pointless task. Still, if you've got the time to kill, then you are certainly free to try.

Some have written, wondering how best to attack them. I have decided that the best weapon to use against this rabble is a sense of humor. Normally, a Christian so dedicated to his religion that he will accost you about yours regards it as some sort of sacred duty. He treats it as something very solemn and sacred.

If you try to debate with him you will get nowhere. In fact, if you argue it will tell him that you regard his childish superstitions as something to be taken seriously, thus puffing him up even more. On the other hand, if you sneer, mock, or laugh at him, show him that you find his beliefs to be too ludicrous to possibly debate seriously, then he will flee the field in search of a more "serious" opponent. Meaning: he wants one who will play along and give him the opportunity to see himself as a sort of crusader for God and all things righteous, one who will validate him. I'd rather not play their game. One definition of "roast" is to severely ridicule. As I said earlier, if a "lamb of God" gets out of line, make "roasted lamb chops."

The trouble is, most of those who are writing to me are so grimly solemn and serious about their "Satanic cause" that they have little sense of humor about it. They take Christianity seriously because they mistakenly see about them a vast cosmic struggle of "Good vs. Evil." Now, while I would definitely agree that the Christians and their ilk have done a truly impressive job of messing things up, and they continue to be a nuisance at times, this certainly does not mean that you should take them seriously. Give serious consideration on how best to deal with the problems they cause and have caused, but you certainly should not play into their hands and boost their already inflated sense of self-importance by treating these ignoramuses and their idiotic beliefs seriously.

For further study I would suggest that you read *The Devil's Notebook* by Anton LaVey (why haven't you already read it?). Pay particular attention to the essays "Let Me Entertain You" and "The Whoopie Cushion Shall Rise Again." Both of these touch upon the vital role a sense of humor plays for every Satanist.

SATANIC VICTIMS?

From time to time, I hear from people who claim to be Satanists, bemoaning the dreadful persecutions that they endure, referring to the medieval witch hunts as a scourge against Satanism that is being restored by modern Christians, and otherwise lamenting the fact that they are being, or at least feel as if they are being, victimized. Since a "Satanic victim culture" is a contradiction in terms, one can only assume that these victims are somewhat lacking in Satanic attributes.

To cite a true example of such thinking, and the parties involved shall remain nameless, some people had their products refused by the shops where they had been printing them. What did they do? Rather than taking their business elsewhere they sat down, proclaimed that they were being victimized and closed up shop. They had other options open which they could have tried but they did not do this.

I have had printers give me a hard time over various things when I was starting to do *From the Pit,* but I did not complain about persecution. I went to a different printer and when he gave me a hard time I went to yet another. I refused to lie down and give up because someone didn't like what I was doing. I refused to behave like a victim. Anyone who does so deserves only our contempt. Amongst the wretched multitudes of herd-things, such victimization is seen as a badge of honor. Amongst us it must be regarded as a stain of shame.

A consistent mark of the victim is that they are constantly complaining about how they are being denied their rights. Such complaints are foolish since it is impossible to deny anyone their rights. Rights are something that you have. They are not what you want to have, or feel that you ought to have. They are not what somebody else says that you should have. A right is something which you are strong enough to keep, or it is that which has been granted to you by those stronger than yourself. In the first case, they cannot be taken from you if you are truly strong enough to hold onto them. In the second case, they are not really yours. They are, in fact, the rights of the stronger power and this power has permitted you to enjoy these rights at their discretion. They can give or take these privileges at will.

Those who complain about being denied their rights are basing their complaint on a philosophy founded on such foolish and abhorrent notions as egalitarianism. To thus complain is tantamount to declaring to the world "I am not a Satanist." "I know my rights!" is the battle cry of the worthless.

Anton LaVey has said that Satanists are born, not made. It is equally true that victims are born rather than made. Satanists are not victims and victims are most certainly not Satanists!

SATANIC BROTHERHOOD?

Having published a Satanic magazine I have received a lot of letters over the years from others professing to be Satanists. In reading these letters I have noticed something which seems to crop up far too many times, something which should not crop up at all. This thing of which I speak is a sense that Satanists should display an all-consuming friendliness and brotherhood towards one another.

Many of those who have written to me have addressed me as "Brother Rose." If you are not one of the children of my parents then don't call me your brother. Let's leave such nonsensical notions of "brotherhood" to the Christians. They have no place in Satanism.

Associated with this is the recurring idea that we Satanists should all be one big happy family, that we should all be friends with one another. Well, I've got some news for you. I don't like all the people who call themselves Satanists. In fact, I positively detest some of them.

There is no rule that says that we all should like each other. That is the kind of stupid idea one would expect a Christian to espouse. This certainly doesn't mean that we must be at one another's throats. It just means that I don't necessarily want to be your friend and it might be best for all concerned to just "live and let live."

A third point that makes its appearance from time to time is the belief that a Satanist should not mock, ridicule or otherwise laugh at another "Satanist." Unfortunately, the definition of Satanist used by such people is so damned broad that just about anybody can be considered a Satanist. This charge of mocking and ridiculing my "brethren" has been leveled at me more than once. The fact of the matter is that a great many so-called "Satanists" spout off so many patently idiotic ideas that it is well-nigh impossible not to laugh at them. I am not about to deny myself the pleasure of laughing at some dimwit merely because he claims to be a Satanist (and some say I'm grim and humorless). Just because you claim to be, or for that matter even if you really are, a Satanist, that doesn't mean that you rate some kind of special consideration from me. I will like whom I wish and laugh at whoever I wish. Aside from a few common ideas, and sometimes these are very few indeed, I do not feel some special bond with *all* other Satanists.

To try to introduce this kind of thinking into Satanism is to fail to grasp one of the key concepts underlying Satanism. Christianity considers the individual as but one part of the collective human whole, part of a single big family. Furthermore, they believe that there is a mystic spiritual bond connecting all Christians and making of them a part of the "Body of Christ." There is no regard for the value of individuality in Christianity. In contrast to such notions, the individual is the foundation of Satanism. We should always regard one another first and foremost as individuals, not as parts of some collective whole.

Whether that collective is race, religion or nationality is beside the point. There is no spiritual bond between Satanists. We are not mere components of some mystical "Body of Satan." We should leave such idiotic notions to lesser creatures. If you subscribe to such ideas perhaps you had better think about whether you too are to be numbered amongst such lesser creatures.

CONFESSIONS OF A LaVEY LACKEY

Over the years I have been criticized for my support of the Church of Satan, and my respect and admiration for Doktor LaVey. Generally this takes the form of being called a lackey, or bootlicker. I would like to address a few points here.

I'm sure that you all have seen some of the diatribes that these assorted wannabees and cuddabeens have put forth. Many have, at some time, been either members of the Church of Satan, or supported it, but a time came when they felt slighted. They will then set about telling everyone that Doktor LaVey was a fraud, a liar, a mere con-man. They will then invite you to follow their new messiah, the "real" messiah of Hell, or join their "evolved" or "first" Satanic Church. The lackey charges invariably come after you reject their invitation; until then they are full of admiration for you.

Some of these people will even dig up every kind word that you ever had to say about them while they were supportive of the Church of Satan as proof of your inconsistency in condemning them now. Inconsistency? If I still say the same thing, and they now say something completely different, which of us is being inconsistent?

Some of these people condemn the alleged arbitrariness of the Church of Satan's decisions. Translation: They thought that they should have been appointed to the Priesthood, but weren't. First off, if you join the Church of Satan because you want to be a Satanic Priest then you are an asshole. I felt deeply honored when Doktor LaVey appointed me to the Priesthood, but that was not my goal in life. Instead, I looked upon it as a pat on the back from a man I had the utmost respect for. To suggest that I had the right to demand that pat on the back is idiotic. Furthermore, while I've heard from some of these jackasses that a Church of Satan Priesthood is meaningless, I would rather have gotten a single kind word from Doktor LaVey than the title of Exalted Unholy Poobah, or whatever the Hell other title they have to offer. I am well aware that in the grand scheme of things a Priesthood in the Church of Satan, in and of itself, doesn't make a Hell of a lot of difference in the world at large. Apparently these people are not. Had they ever gotten the Priesthood they so craved most would've considered it a license to be an utterly obnoxious asshole in all their dealings with others. There's a lesson there for those with eyes to see.

Another common avenue of attack is to charge that members of the Church of Satan worshipped Dr. LaVey. These dolts cannot distinguish worship from respect. Their kind are usually possessed of such weak egos that they are incapable of showing anyone respect. They can grasp the idea of worshiping some exalted "other," but to show respect to another person is alien to them. They feel diminished by such a sense of respect. Their method of attack reveals their worshipful nature. They imagine that by criticizing Dr. LaVey they can diminish, or cause us to reject, the Church of Satan. They do not attack the philosophy; they attack the philosopher. This makes it quite clear that it is they who are the personality cultists. When the man disappointed them they turned against him. Obviously the philosophy meant nothing to them. While I respected Dr. LaVey, nothing associated with his personal life could cause me to reject the philosophy he set forth and the Church he established. I've never believed any of the tired accusations that these people have made, but even if every one of them were true it would not change a single word in *The Satanic Bible*. The Church of Satan would still remain. Because these people chose to worship a god that did not reward them in what they felt was an appropriate manner they turned away, consumed with bitterness. Good riddance, we don't need them.

Doktor LaVey blazed a trail. We who followed him because we were traveling the same way will continue undeterred. Let the weaklings and fools fall away. As we climb higher more will certainly fall away. It is the way of things. I would encourage everyone to sit down and think about what their motivations are. If you are on this road for the wrong reasons then by all means, jump to the rocks below. Just don't invite me to jump along with you; I've got better things to do.

RITUAL TO SECURE COOPERATION

Many people have written to me bemoaning their inability to get their local bookstores to order books for them. I am well aware of the fact that there are many incompetents out there. Generally though, these people are not bemoaning the incompetence of bookstore employees. No, they say that the problem is that people react to them in a hostile manner and will not cooperate with them.

Normally there are sufficient clues in their letters to deduce the fact that they bring this lack of cooperation on their own heads. An application of the principles of Lesser Magic would remedy the situation quite handily. Alas, they seem reluctant to use Lesser Magic. What follows is a ritual designed to address this situation and secure the needed cooperation. With slight modifications this ritual can also be used to address other, similar situations.

Requirements for Ritual

- Standard ritual gear as per *The Satanic Bible*
- Plenty of floor space in ritual chamber (padding on the floor might be helpful)
- A small whip or scourge
- Begin the ritual with "purification of the air" as per *The Satanic Bible*

The Invocation

CELEBRANT: In the name of all the Lords of the Abyss, I call out to the Powers of Darkness. Come to my aid for I am helpless before my adversaries. I am thy servant. Thy will is as my own. I am ever dutiful in serving thee. Come forth from thy dark abodes and answer to your names. Hear my plea.
Oh hear the names...

At this point the appropriate names are called out, the elixir is drunk, and the Four Princes called forth. The following invocation is now read:

CELEBRANT: Hear me Lord Satan! I am persecuted on all sides. My enemies hem me in and would set out to cut me off. They would deny me goods and services because I serve thee, O Dark Prince.

The celebrant should now throw himself to the floor, and with arms and legs flailing cry out:

It's not fair! It's not fair! It's not fair!

This should continue until the celebrant seems thoroughly purged. It is possible that tears will flow during this part of the rite. If so, give way to this emotion fully.

By this time the celebrant should realize what a whiny asshole he has been. He should now stand and face the altar and take up his whip or scourge. Taking the scourge in his left hand he must whip himself 9 times. He should then turn to the south and say:

Lord Satan. I've been an asshole. I will no longer be such a whiny bastard.

As he says this he should bring the scourge down across his back 9 more times. He should repeat this procedure apologizing to all Four Princes. The celebrant should then meditate for a moment on the lessons of this ritual. After a period of contemplation the celebrant should go forth to order the book, keeping in mind the basic principles of Lesser Magic. After you have successfully ordered the book, return to your ritual chamber, read the "Twelfth Enochian Key" and finish it by saying:

So it is done!

LIES I LEARNED IN SCHOOL

School days—what a nightmare! If anything could turn you against the education system then passing through it should do the trick. I thought that I'd share with you just a little of the bullshit that I was taught in school.

Man is the Most Highly Evolved Animal

Is that so? This is the kind of thing that too many otherwise intelligent people fall for. I suppose that there is an element of vanity in that. As deflating as it may be to one's vanity, this is quite simply untrue. Man has evolved, and continues to evolve, just as everything else does.

Evolution is a constant in this world of Heraclitean flux. This evolution is sometimes in the form of positive adaptation; other times it takes the form of maladaptation. Man is no more highly evolved than are horses, dogs, apes or even viruses. It could even be said that man is less successfully evolved, or more poorly adapted to his environment, than are a great many other life forms. This whole idea that man is somehow at the pinnacle of evolution as a byproduct of residual Christian attitudes seeping into the study of evolution. Evolution thus acquires a goal, a purpose. It becomes the means by which God creates the world, and places man at he pinnacle of that creation.

Well it just ain't that way.

Evolution has no goal or purpose other than adaptation, for good or ill. We're just along for the ride, adapting right alongside of everything else. People have generally come to an acceptance of the idea that man has evolved, but they just cannot accept the idea that man is "just another animal"; my teachers were no exceptions.

Democracy is the Ideal Form of Government

The big lie! Sometimes I think that the central function of education is to indoctrinate children with this abominable notion. It seems plain to me that democratic ideas are always put forward during the decline of a civilization. Democracy is a reaction to the exhaustion of a culture. As hard as it may be to believe, I have been told that without democracy, neither great art nor scientific advances are possible. Needless to say, my teachers were hardly pleased when I asked about the artistic and scientific achievements of such ancient non-democratic societies as Egypt, Mesopotamia, Persia, Rome, China, Japan, and Renaissance Italy. It was during my school years that I was first introduced to the childish practice of tarring those who dare question the perfection of democratic institutions with the name of fascist. I was considered a rotten Nazi bastard just because I had the temerity to question this, the central lie of the modern age (although the fact that I would occasionally hum the *Horst Wessel Lied* didn't help matters any). Things haven't changed much.

Mass Movements of "The People" are the Motivating Forces of History

This is one of the stupidest things I ever heard. At first I thought that the history teacher who taught me this was being sarcastic. Amazingly enough, he was quite serious. My disdain for him was matched by his for me. He thought that my thinking was hopelessly obsolete because I categorically rejected his silly beliefs.

Contrary to the egalitarian, populist, democratic ideology that would postulate such an absurdity, the plain fact is that history has always been made by strong individuals. Even the mass movements which this idiot of a teacher placed so much stock in are not the work of *the people.* Mass movements are invariably centered around the leadership of a strong individual, or a coterie of such individuals. Without such leadership or guidance the masses will never move. I believe that it was H.L. Mencken who said that William the Conqueror was more important than everyone else of his generation. Today the thinking probably goes like this instead: the people of Normandy wanted to conquer England so they chose William to lead the invasion, and rewarded him by making him king. Pardon me while I laugh uproariously.

Picasso was a Great Artist

You have got to be kidding! Have you seen a Picasso? When they got around to introducing my "peers" and I to the world of art, I was taught that the greatest artists were Picasso, Andy Warhol, and other such modern hacks. DaVinci, Michelangelo, and Rembrandt were glossed over as old fashioned and obsolete. Many other real artists were not even mentioned while every dimwit who dribbled paint on a canvas was given an obscene excess of adulation. As far as my teachers, if they can be graced with that name, were concerned everyone prior to the advent of abstract art is worthless and might well be consigned to the flames. I should think that quite the opposite would be more true.

I have often been asked about my education; as if that had anything at all to do with intelligence, or learning.

Education is just indoctrination. The possession of a diploma or degree means only that you have learned what they want you to know. If you want to know something you are better off learning it for yourself. On the other hand, if you want people to think that you know something then by all means, get all the "education" that can be had. Just don't think that you'll necessarily come out of the system with any real knowledge or understanding.

BITTER FRUIT

Recently I was pleased to see that my home state of Alabama, though it's a bit backwards at times, has taken the lead in once more making prison a place of punishment rather than rehabilitation or resocialization. Earlier this year the prison commissioner had the prisoners' cable TV cut off. Now he has reinstated the use of chain gangs and has ordered that space which was to be used as gymnasiums in new prisons under construction should be used instead for housing prisoners. I suspect that the bleeding hearts will be going to court *en mass* in an effort to end such "barbaric" practices. The first convicts to be assigned to the chain gangs have already complained of how degrading and dehumanizing the practice is, even before they have even been put to work. The only reply such whining deserves is the answer that the Shadow gave to such scum in the immortal radio show of a bygone era—"The weed of crime bears bitter fruit!"

If there is any lesson to be drawn from the "enlightened" penal policies of the last several decades it is that the best way to handle criminals is with a harshness commensurate with their crimes. Coddling criminals in prison will only produce habitual criminals.

There has been altogether too much concern shown over the welfare of prisoners in this society. These bleeding hearts will often say things like "you can tell a lot about a society by the way they treat their prisoners", implying that only barbarians would be so cruel as to treat criminals with anything other than mercy and loving-kindness. Well, they are half right. You *can* tell a lot about a society by the way they treat their criminals. A society that treats them as anything other than enemies is a weak society; a society that is sliding downhill into a much deserved destruction.

As I mentioned earlier, the use of chain gangs, or other forms of forced labor, is a positive step. Rather than simply sending prisoners off to be warehoused we should make them be self supporting through their labor. As an example, prison farms should grow the food prisoners eat. Only an idiot would argue that prisoners need, or should have, cable TV, gymnasiums or top quality medical care.

The issue of prisoners' health care has been too long neglected. Not long ago a prisoner got an organ transplant at public expense just because he was in prison when the need for it arose. More recently I heard about a convicted child molester who received a penile implant at public expense. WHY? That is madness! As far as I'm concerned, anything beyond minor, temporary, care, such as setting a broken bone, should be denied them. If they will die without major, or long term, medical treatment then they will just die. Such measures will provide an incentive to stay out of prison.

The current state of affairs regarding capital punishment is a joke. A prisoner sentenced to death today might end up dying of old age before ever facing the executioner. Furthermore those who do meet the executioner are probably going to die by some "humane", and expensive, means such as lethal injection. The whole system relating to capital punishment must be thrown out. I think that the old Soviet system had much to recommend it. It was a very heavily politicized system of course, but the idea behind it was sound.

I would suggest the following system: after the initial conviction a case will receive two independent judicial reviews, not full trials. Any new evidence can be submitted at this point. If both uphold the conviction then the prisoner dies that day, if there is a split decision a final judicial review is carried out. The means of execution should be much simpler than such options as lethal injection, electrocution or the gas chamber. Hanging is a possibility, but I think that decapitation would be more effective psychologically. An individual might be much more horrified and fearful if facing the prospect of such a death. The best death for such riff-raff is neither of these options though. That old Roman standby, crucifixion, is almost ideal. It is a long, drawn out, painful death. Just the thing to inspire fear, and that is after all what it's all about.

It is true that there are many people in prison who, as far as

I'm concerned, should not be. Strictly moral offenses should not be considered criminal. A whole host of things, such as prostitution, the use and sale of various drugs, possession of firearms, etc., should be decriminalized. Do not think I am turning a blind eye towards genuine crime. If a drug addict steals or commits crimes under the influence then he should be considered criminal but in and of itself the fact that he or she used drugs, or owned a gun or whatever else is irrelevant. When your actions involve only yourself and willing partners then they are nobody's business but your own.

After a suitable revision of the law books we must recognize criminals as nothing less than an enemy. As it says in *The Satanic Bible*, "Hate your enemies with a whole heart, and if a man smite you on one cheek, smash him on the other! ...Make yourself a terror to your adversary!" I could go on but you get the point. The criminal does not fear the sword of justice anymore. They must once again learn to know that fear. They must be made to understand that punishment is swift and certain. They must learn that we don't care whether they are rehabilitated and resocialized. All that matters is that they know that we will not sit idly by and watch them trample over all that we have built. Let them tremble in the shadow of the strong and remember the kiss of our lash. We must crush them beneath our heel without pity or remorse. They *must* be dominated, and the only effective way to do this is to make them fear our wrath.

Such a day is coming. Gradually, in fits and starts, this society is coming to the realization that the status quo isn't working. Only fear can keep crime in check. Pity for "poor underprivileged young people drawn into a life of crime" has only allowed criminals to put their knives to our throats. That pity is finally dying, and none too soon I might add. Harshness is more and more often the thing people call for. Society would see an end to the perks and benefits of prison life. It would see a return to punishment. Perhaps some day soon the criminal element will be forced to eat that bitter fruit.

MAYBE IT'S NOT SO BITTER AFTER ALL

Recently I commented favorably on what I thought was a positive trend in the penal policies of my native Alabama. The cornerstone of the new "get tough" policy was to be the resurrection of the chain gang. Well, I have now had a chance to observe some of the implementation of these policies. It turns out that the bitter fruit isn't quite as bitter as it ought to be.

A few months ago I had the opportunity to observe these "inhumane" and "brutal" policies in action. A gang of convicts were "working" by the highway. Actually, it looked to me more like a lot of guys standing around in the grass. It was determined that forcing them to work when they were tired would be inhumane. As a consequence there is no motivation for this collection of assorted human filth to exert themselves. So they stand around in the sun for a few hours, periodically calling their guard to dispatch a snake for them. The only remotely positive thing in the new chain gang policy is that some of these creatures find the very idea of it degrading. This at least injects some further slight element of negative reinforcement into the prison experience. I doubt if these trifling indignities will be sufficient to truly dissuade anybody from criminal behavior though. There was an element of the policy that did seem useful, but it has since come under fire from various apologists for the poor, underprivileged victims of the criminal justice system. This single bright spot in the whole sorry mess was the policy of locking troublemakers to a bar about five feet off the ground all day. This required him to stand, or hang from the wrists, all day long. I doubt that this will last much longer, in fact, it may already be a thing of the past. I hear that some in the state legislature are trying to implement phase two of this get tough policy. Phase two is to be the introduction of caning to the penal codes. Having seen the pitiful results of the chain gang policy I can only imagine that this caning will consist of, at worst, a sharp rap across the back of the hand with a wooden ruler. I can almost feel the tremors as the criminals shake in their boots... .with uncontrolled spasms of laughter.

I know that there were several other states which were considering implementing a chain gang policy. It is possible that one or more of them will manifest a strength and resolve which Alabama lacked. The fact that a punishment is cruel should be no mark against it, in fact it should be seen as something positive. Amongst the assorted stupidities of the great democratic scriptures the rule against cruel and unusual punishment has to be one of the stupidest. It is the very cruelty of punishment that acts as a conditioning element, that provides the negative reinforcement to overcome the positive reinforcements provided by the satisfactions and gains of criminality. As for unusualness, that is what causes the mind to remember the pain inflicted upon him through the cruelties of his jailers. New, and ever more unusual sufferings must be inflicted upon recalcitrant criminals. A good day of cruel and unusual punishment is worth much more than a few years of jail time. Unfortunately, it looks as if this society is too weak to accept this simple fact. It prefers its humanitarian pipe dreams and marches headlong into the maw of destruction singing about the basic goodness of man, the feasibility of rehabilitating the criminals, and insisting that kindness will make everything better. It is a parade of fools which knows no equal and I always enjoy seeing some such deluded fool come running up against the harsh realities of things. Their wails are sure to warm the cockles of my black heart as they bemoan their rude awakening to the truth. Alas, too few truly learn the lesson and will soon convince themselves that their brush with reality was merely an aberration. As 1 said, they are fools. I wish upon them all a full measure of suffering.

I will close by quoting H.L. Mencken, these lines were written in 1928, and things have only gotten worse. "There was a time when imprisonment was a rare punishment. Men were thrown into jails to await trial, but when they were tried at last they were commonly punished in other ways. Some were put to death. Others were deported. Others were flogged. Others lost certain civil rights. Yet others were mutilated.

But all these various and protean punishments were eventually outlawed by the humanitarians... hangings grow rare, and flogging is seldom heard of. No one is mutilated any more. No one is deported, at least in America. One and all, large and small, professionals and accidentals, men who run afoul of the law are cast into cages, and there held at the disposal of morons." And still the parade of fools marches blithely on.

ART?

A couple of months ago I saw something in a newspaper about the latest doings of what passes for an artist these days. This man had the German Reichstag covered in a glorified tarp and called it art. Once upon a time a certain degree of talent was required to make a name for one's self as an artist. It would seem to me that talent is no longer seen as a prerequisite for an artist.

What a sad state we have come to when any kind of stupidity can be called art and some damned fool will believe it. Wrap a building in a tarp and it is high art; put a bucket of shit on a table and "Behold! a masterpiece"; smear menstrual blood on a canvas and you are hailed as DaVinci's superior. This sad state of affairs is the triumph of egalitarianism. Everyone can be a great artist. Anybody who has the gall to suggest that this pseudo-artistic bullshit is just that will be vilified as elitist and reactionary. To think that a painting or sculpture should actually look like something is almost unheard of.

Aggravating this egalitarian nonsense is the welfare state ethos which expects the state to provide a blank check for "the arts". The suggestion that public monies should not be used to subsidize anything that might be called art, and that could be just about anything, is met by such a wailing and moaning from these alleged artists that you would think that art would be without public funding. What is forgotten, or perhaps forgotten is the wrong word since most of the dimwits making up the population are quite ignorant about almost everything except what they see on TV, is that the greatest achievements in art were made without such lavish public expenditures. The great artists of the renaissance worked under a rather novel system. It was called patronage.

Patronage was a very simple system. You are paid to produce what your patron wants. If you don't want to do that you don't have to, but of course you won't get paid for doing what you want to do. This system was not an obstacle to the best artists since they were often able to find ways to express their own artistic will while producing what their patrons wanted. Given their distinct lack of real talent it is easy to see why modern artists fear the return of the patronage system. However, without such a system we will continue to be plagued by modern art that looks like nothing, performance artists who expect to be paid for behaving idiotically and an assortment of excrement, garbage and tarp covered structures all masquerading as art.

HOW TO BE A SATANIC BREEDER

Much has been written in the past about "Satanic Breeders". According to the fevered imaginings of fundamentalist Christians there are women whose only purpose is to produce children for the purpose of ritual sacrifice. Of course, all of this has precisely nothing to do with real Satanism. However, there is a place in a Satanic society for what could be termed a "Satanic Breeder". In this article I will explain just what I mean.

There are a great many women in the world who seem to have but one goal in life, to produce as many children as they possibly can. Unfortunately such women seldom produce offspring of any real value. What I propose is a specialized class of slavery, or to use a modern euphemism, a new service industry. What I propose is not entirely new. There have been many tentative approaches to it but nobody has really considered it as a large scale operation and to my knowledge no one has considered it in quite these terms.

Many couples of the aristocratic master caste might wish to have children but, for whatever the reason, do not want to produce them in the "usual way." Under this system the sort of women who currently produce great masses of children of dubious value would be utilized as a resource. These generally useless women would be permitted to do what they want to do; bear children. These children, the children of aristocratic parents, would be implanted in these women as embryos. In return for bearing the children of masters, these women would be cared for by the parents throughout their pregnancy. Unlike the surrogate mothers we have today, these women will not have the option of keeping the child they carry. They are not to be regarded as mothers, or "birth mothers" as the modern expression has it. They are just wombs. Some might be retained as wet nurses but this is rather doubtful as it would be quite unwise to do anything to foster maternal feelings in these women. They must become their functions so long as they serve as breeders. They must see themselves as breeders, baby producers not mothers.

The same conditions would apply to this specialized class of slaves that I would apply to any other slaves with one exception. With all other slave groups I would stress that, with few exceptions, slavery is a path which an individual chooses, an that individual could leave slavery behind at any time they are prepared to take responsibility for themselves. Amongst these breeders the only stipulation to that rule would be that they cannot opt to leave their servitude if they are pregnant. Furthermore, if the breeder acts to terminate the pregnancy on her own she should be given to the parents that they might exact whatever vengeance they see fit. Aside from that the breeder should be governed by the same general rules applying to slavery.

I want to make clear that I do not think that breeders should be used by those who are themselves unable to have children. Technology has made it possible for such people to have children through third parties but I'm not all sure that this is a good idea. If you are unable to bear children without a lot of high tech tinkering then that might be natures way of saying don't breed. Who knows what sort of genetic anomalies are creeping into the gene pool through such interventions? I would intend that this service be used so as to make it possible for healthy, productive individuals to reproduce without the risks and lost productivity which pregnancy could bring about.

DON'T DRUG THAT MONKEY

Lately I've been listening to some arguments, both for and against, the use of animals for pharmaceutical research. Both sides seem to be basing their arguments on either idiotic assumptions or flagrant emotionalism. There is no way that this rank jungle of wrong-headedness can be brought under control. Its time for some rather heavy handed clear cutting.

On the one hand you have the opponents of animal research. I must confess that while I am instinctively drawn to their side of things, their approach is so muddleheaded and stupid that I cannot give my support to them. There are two basic arguments. Some use one of them while others use both. Argument number one goes something like this. Animals have the same fundamental and inalienable rights as people do. Since animals have rights it is wrong to use them for experimentation. Argument number two can not be articulated intelligently because it is meant to totally bypass the intellect. It is demonstrated by holding up a picture of a puppy or a baby monkey in the hopes of activating the instinctive mechanisms that cause us to want to protect our young. It often works with non-human babies because there are certain common infantile traits in many mammals which can trigger these protective responses.

On the other hand you have the advocates of animal research. Their arguments are mirror images of those of their opponent's. Argument number one is that there is an inalienable human right to life. They do not believe that animals have any such rights. Argument number two is much like the second argument of the animal rights types. It consists of holding up pictures of sick children who, according to them, can only be saved through animal testing.

What can you say to such doggedly persistent stupidity? My initial response is to say "Let pharmaceutical research be damned. Let a plague take the lot"; however, that would be throwing the baby out with the bathwater. Instead, let us try and look at this whole issue reasonably. I will not try to argue against either side's approach number two. As I have already mentioned, this approach is designed to bypass the intellect entirely. It has to do this because it has no merit. Such rank emotionalism is quite unnecessary to make a point. As for point number one, both side make certain foolish assumptions. One side errs in asserting that animals have inalienable rights, the other errs in it's assumption that humans have them. As I've said before, the belief in inherent and inalienable rights is nothing but a modern superstition. Any conclusions arrived at through such reasoning will be tainted by this groundless foolishness. It is possible to argue intelligently against the use of animal testing for pharmaceutical research. To do so requires an abandonment of some of those modern superstitions.

It has always seemed silly to me that drugs intended for human use are tested on non-human subjects. Instead of testing drugs on a progression of animal subjects, rats, dogs then monkeys or whatever progression is to be used, why not be more direct about it, cut out the middle-monkey as it were. Since all drugs must be ultimately tested on human subjects anyway, why not use humans for preliminary testing as well. There is certainly no shortage of prisoners, lunatics, or indigents pissing on street corners. These are the proper subjects for research. Would it not be better to bring meaning and purpose to the miserable lives of this wretched vermin than to senselessly kill even one animal?

The humanitarians would argue that to use these people as test subjects is a violation of their human rights etc. etc. ad nauseum. I told you we were going to have to rid ourselves of some of these modern superstitions. It comes down to a question of valuations. What is more valuable, a cure for AIDs, cancer or some other disease, or a few hundred parasitic humans? If you say that these parasites have a greater value than such discoveries then you are truly a fool and I can only hope that you die screaming in pain from some horrid pestilence. A further benefit of such a course is that the society would no longer be burdened with such parasites. Many will no doubt die in the course of research, those that live will continue to be useful research subjects until their luck runs out and they too are sacrificed on the altar of science.

Only in this way can these creatures be made useful.

In *Macbeth,* William Shakespeare wrote "As hounds and greyhounds, mongrels, spaniels, curs, shoughs, water-rugs and demi-wolves are clept all by the name of dogs: the valued file distinguishes the swift, the slow, the subtle, the housekeeper, the hunter, every one according to the gift which bounteous nature hath in him closed, whereby he does receive particular addition, from the bill that writes them all alike: and so of men." This passage illustrates a bit of ancient wisdom that people today seem to do their best to forget. There is a difference in inherent value between one man and another. Some men are of great value in the world. Others can only be made valuable by throwing their lives away in some worthwhile endeavor. If the cure for cancer can be had through the loss of a few thousand, a few hundred thousand, or even millions of prisoners, lunatics or other good-for-nothings then I'd call that one hell of a bargain.

'TIS THE SEASON TO BE STUPID

Yes, it's that time of year again. People pack themselves like sardines into malls to pay inflated sale prices, they put up with bell ringing beggars and, in short, think and behave quite idiotically. It is appropriate that a particularly stupid new holiday should be celebrated at this time of year.

Kwanzaa was invented in 1966* so that blacks could celebrate African culture. I don't mind people inventing holidays; hell, somebody's got to invent the damned things. I do have a problem with people inventing stupid ones. The problem with Kwanzaa is twofold. First, it celebrates something that doesn't exist, and never existed, and second, it promotes an ethic of collective responsibility.

It may not be politically correct to say it, but there is no "African culture" to celebrate. Sub-Saharan Africa never developed anything even approaching a unified culture. Kwanzaa also emphasizes that there is a sort of communal obligation between all blacks. That each must be "his brother's keeper". Kwanzaa is a misguided effort to make people feel good about themselves for the most trivial of reasons, in this case because their ancestors were Africans. I suppose it does give meaning to empty lives, although anyone who needs this to make their lives meaningful should by all means kill themselves. Oh well, 'tis the season… … .

---

* *Author's note*—I suppose the best way to think about it is in light of the eternal balance. In order for the Church of Satan to come forth a certain quantity of shit had to come as well. Kwanzaa is just part of that requisite load of shit.

ON THE USES OF FASCISM

A short while back I got the most amusing bit of mail. The sender of this "letter" did not sign it, or give a return address so I don't know who it was. The note, written in a childish scrawl upon a torn bit of notebook paper emblazoned with a dozen or so swastikas and double sig runes, gloated that the *"whig-liberals"* had lost and the fascists had won the power struggle within the CoS. It further advised me to "get on the winning side or get left behind". My first response to this bit of idiocy was a good laugh at this idiot's expense. Later, I felt a bit of mild annoyance creeping in. My annoyance came because I am really getting tired of this little tempest in a teapot about fascism.

The writer of this note admonishes me to choose sides. With all *due* respect, I will decline to do so. The reason for this is simple. The whole fascist vs libertarians issue is, in fact, a non-issue. I stand above the sort of childishly dualistic mentality revealed by those who cling to this nonsensical dispute.

The partisans of both sides of this thing need to think about why they want to cling so tenaciously to their half of this little either/or affair. Haven't they realized that with just a little bit of thought they can convert limited either/or options into much broader and/or options much of the time, or is thought something so alien to them that they cannot even imagine it?

Part of the problem, I think, is that the partisans of both sides are forgetting about stratification. The principal thrust of the dispute is, as I see it, a question of social order. Any social order worth a damn will have a trapezoidal organization. In other words, it will have a small elite at the top, and a broad and largely undifferentiated mass at the bottom. In between there will be others ranging from the near-elites to the near-mass types with the relative numbers of these shrinking as you approach the elites. There is no one-size-fits-all answer.

Those who cling to extremely liberal/libertarian positions are thinking solipsistically. They do not consider that liberal attitudes will not permit the elites to effectively rule the mass, and make no mistake, it must be ruled. Those who cling to the all fascism-all the time view are fools. They do not think about the fact that as you rise within the social order two things happen; the first is that the degree of individuality increases, and the second is that the degree of self control increases so that external control becomes increasingly unnecessary, and unwanted. If it were applied at the higher levels, fascism would be as disastrous as excessive liberalism would be at the bottom.

I will admit that fascism could be a very effective means of controlling the masses. It is not the only way, but it is one of the quickest and easiest. The degree of individuality at the lower levels is often negligible anyway, so fusing them all into a single group mind, to be manipulated as needed by the elites is not at all unfeasible. In fact, the masses will probably thank you for bringing meaning and purpose into their wretched little lives. However, as you move up within the social hierarchy you will start to find it more and more difficult to implement a fascist order. The best solution to this would be to use fascism where you can. When you begin to notice a fairly strong resistance you change the program. You no longer try to fuse these people with the mass at the bottom. You give them a different mass-mind to relate to. In short, you turn them into middle management. Leave them the tiresome task of administering to this mass on a day to day basis. The orders come down from on high, the middle class asserts its superiority in goading the mass into carrying out the will of the elites. As you rise out of the middle classes you will start to find those who have no particular desire to put on their uniforms & badges and lord it over the proles. As you enter this strata you must recognize that increasing freedom, to be coupled with increasing responsibility of course, will get better results. Remember, elites must be free to create, the masses must be enslaved that they might be given direction, but in between lies the grey area that black and white distinctions invariably miss, and yet, this grey area must be accounted for.

The error of the entrenched advocates of fascism & libertarianism is that they mistake means for ends. We live in a complex world. To see life as a series of simple either/or choices is quite foolish. There exists a vast range of options between these stark and simplistic dualities. Learn to think beyond the dualities... .if you can.

TO BE, OR NOT TO BE...EVIL

I have gotten letters from people who felt that they weren't evil enough, or who thought that I was not evil enough. What is evil? Think about it. Evil is one of *their* words. The Satanist should be, to use Nietzsche's phrase, beyond good and evil. If you think that I haven't been evil enough I have some news for you. I have never tried to be evil. In fact, I have never given a moment of thought to whether something I said or did was evil. It simply doesn't matter to me. I have some more news for you. I even listen to "Christian" music from time to time.

I'm not talking about gospel music. That stuff is pure shit. I'm talking about the requiems and masses of Bach, Beethoven, Berlioz, Verdi, Bruckner and others. I also find Stravinsky's Symphony of Psalms quite enjoyable. Does this make me a traitor to Satanism? Some of the exquisitely idiotic creatures who have written to me over the years would say "yes". If you are in that camp I would encourage you to think for a change. Think about the difference between the ugly, simplistic, abject, base and wretched nature of gospel music and the beauty, complexity and grandeur of, for example, Berlioz's Requiem. There is no comparison. If you can divide the world into two camps the Christian/Chandala rabble and the Satanic masters then gospel music is the creation of the former, the great masses of the latter.

The bottom line is this. Do not worry about being evil enough, or counting the sins you've committed. When you do that you are playing the Christian's game. Dedicate yourself to joy, and to beauty. If you find pleasure in listening to Bach's Mass in B Minor, or looking at a wonderful old gothic cathedral or anything else that might be considered "Christian" do not apologize for it. Admire these things for their beauty. Rejoice in the pleasure they provide to you in the here and now. What is more Satanic than joy? Don't allow yourself to he limited by those who cannot feel joy without guilt. If the rabble must be confined to guilty pleasures then let us revel in guiltless ones, whatever they may be.

THE CHRISTIANS ARE COMING! *OR ARE THEY?*

There are a great many people who call themselves Satanists that seem to think that the advent of a Christian theocratic republic of America is imminent. This is unfortunate. Once upon a time I may have permitted myself the belief that those who professed to be Satanists were quite above such ideas. My dealings with my fellow Satanists over the last several years has done a very thorough job of disabusing me of this notion.

This foolish notion is born out of two things. The first is an all too ready acceptance of televised images as a reflection of reality. The second is an acceptance of political rhetoric as a reflection of reality. Both of these things are errors.

It is certainly true that various Christian media personalities are fond of dabbling in politics. It is also true that there are a great many politicians who voice their support of the fundamentalist Christian agenda in their speeches. When an election is going on there is always an increase in this rhetoric. The important thing to consider is not what is said, but rather, what is done.

It is useful to consider a few of the realities here. Politicians need to present media images of enthusiastic, and adoring, supporters. These images are used to activate the clustering instinct. When the herd sees images of mass support they are more likely to go along with it. It is much easier to inspire highly emotional, even frenzied, support among the weak minded. Politicians of the left always use the parasitic socialistic mass for this purpose. Politicians of the right tend to use the fundamentalist Christians.

The nature of the process, as well as of these particular groups, guarantees that while you can promise whatever you need to in order to inspire the requisite degree of adoration you will not have to deliver on any of those promises. As this is about the alleged Christian threat I'll limit myself to them. Every fundamentalist Christian I have ever dealt with was a firm believer in the idea that in the years prior to the second coming the forces of evil would reign on earth. This belief provides for the enterprising politician the perfect excuse.

Consider this scenario. Mr. X is running for a senatorial seat. He goes to a large church or religious rally and promises the Christians that he'll give them everything they want. School prayer, criminalizing abortions, TV censorship, etc. The Christian rabble is convinced that Mr. X is a fine, upstanding Christian and applaud him enthusiastically. The media broadcasts a clip of this enthusiastic crowd, and Mr. X uses it in his advertising. Other sheep see this rabid enthusiasm and decide to go along with the crowd. Mr. X becomes senator X. As senator, X puts forth some extreme proposal which is certain to fail. After it fails he goes on to the usual business of lining his pockets. The only measures that get passed are those that enrich politicians and/or their flunkies, or those that have broad appeal like giving away increasingly worthless money through "entitlements". Senator X goes home. He tells his more mainstream constituents about the free handouts and assorted other goodies that he's secured for them. He then goes back to the Christians and says "I tried, but the Devil's minions are opposing me. Stand behind me and I'll continue to oppose the forces of evil." The Christians interpret this as proof that Jesus is coming soon and enthusiastically applaud Senator X. This cycle can be repeated again and again.

I will concede that fundamentalists elected to local offices can be, and often are, a pain in the ass. These fanatical jackasses usually do not last long. The policies which they introduce are usually both foolish and unworkable. They are also usually thrown out by the courts or done away with by later politicians. Contrary to popular belief the vast majority of people do not want Christian fundamentalism forced upon them.

Christian fundamentalism, like all of the other forms of fundamentalism, are manifestations of a religion's death. All of the non-fundamentalist Christian sects are essentially neutralized, with the exception of Roman Catholicism which is a weed that grows best in backwards, third-world, havens of ignorance.

Support for the Christian agenda is also vastly overestimated. Many might superficially agree with their calls for renewed morality. The difference is that while to the fundamentalist Christian morality means living strictly in accordance with biblical teachings, to most people it just has a nice sound to it. To the masses it just means that you should wear a good-guy badge all the time. They are too busy enjoying their "bread and circuses" -entitlements and TV—to worry about the strict biblical asceticism advocated by the fundamentalists.

So, the next time you are tempted to worry about the coming theocracy just sit down, relax, think about this and move on to more important things. Do not waste your time thinking that the Christians are coming. They're not. They're going.

A BETTER PLACE

In the past I have written about what is wrong with the currently dominant governmental system—Egalitarian Democracy. What I have not done is to spell out exactly what I would like to see replace it. I have been called everything from a nihilist to a nazi by my detractors. Largely this is because I have used, in allusions to what I'd like to see come to be, such emotionally charged words as aristocracy, masters, slaves, domination.

Many people are apparently unable to see beyond the stigma which the forces of egalitarianism have placed upon these words. To them they are just buzzwords. I've also been criticized on the grounds that I am tearing down without building up. This is a notoriously idiotic idea which, unfortunately, is all too common. (I would recommend H.L.Mencken's essay "The Cult of Hope" in his *Prejudices: Second Series* to all who hold such views, or have been plagued by those who do.) I am not writing this for my critics. I learned long ago that you shouldn't try to justify yourself to your critics. No, I'm writing this because I believe that it will clarify some of my ideas. The ideas set forth in this series represent an ideal of a sort. My ideal. I am well aware of the fact that social engineering is not particularly reliable, and I am not saying that this is how it will be. I'm sure it won't be just like this. What I am doing is making suggestions about a direction in which I'd like to see the society travel. It is my "Utopia", although many would no doubt find it quite dystopian. It is merely a dream of a better place.

The Aristocracy

One of the terms I use fairly often is *aristocracy.* This word is pretty much guaranteed to trigger a negative response in people raised in, and conditioned by, an egalitarian society. Even those who are able to move beyond the social conditioning of their youth are often unable to think of an aristocracy in any other sense than it was used during the age of the hereditary, "*divine right*" type aristocracies or, to put it more accurately, pseudo-aristocracies of the past. This is *not* what I have in mind. When I use the word I am referring to an elite of capable, responsible, and intelligent individuals. This, to me, is aristocracy; the only true aristocracy. Nothing less is deserving of the name.

This kind of aristocracy would be open ended. It would embrace any who were worthy, and it would cast out those who were not. No artificial impediments would keep the capable and responsible out, nor would there be any props to keep the irresponsible and incompetent safely ensconced in its ranks. The central rule is this-You are responsible for what you do, and will be held accountable. If you can't accept 100% accountability, full responsibility for taking care of yourself, then you aren't aristocratic material. If you need someone to take care of you, and protect you from yourself and others then you are fit only to be a slave.

At the highest levels of society a state of near anarchy would prevail. I do not use this word in the sense that most people would understand it. What I mean is that the aristocracy would consist of those people who are capable of self-rule. The aristocracy would enjoy a maximum of personal freedom. Control will come from within. Any member of the aristocracy incapable of such self-rule will be cast out into the ranks of the slaves. The lower orders, those who are incapable of such self-rule, who need to be guided and controlled, will be dominated by the members of the aristocracy. What government there is will not be by the people, for the people, and of the people but would instead be by the aristocracy, of the aristocracy and for the masses. The precise hierarchies in such a system would have to be sorted out as needed.

An aristocracy of the sort that I am talking about is a far more natural kind of social organization. It does not require the kind of interminable bureaucracy which is found everywhere today. Under such a system the state, as it exists today, would dwindle almost into oblivion. I will address government and the state in a later installment in this series.

H.L. Mencken wrote eloquently about this aristocratic anarchy in his excellent book *The Philosophy of Friedrich Nietzsche*. He said "To the average American or Englishman the very name of anarchy causes a shudder, because it invariably conjures up a picture of a land terrorized by low-browed assassins with matted beards, carrying bombs in one hand and mugs of beer in the other. But, as a matter of fact, there is no reason to believe that, if all laws were abolished tomorrow, such swine would survive the day."

Slavery

Not everyone is cut out for the aristocracy. The non-aristocratic masses I lump together under the name of slave. By using the word slave I do not suggest a return to old style chattel slavery. There will be no whips and chains for they will not be needed. The slaves in this aristocratic society would want their slavery. I once heard it said that the price of freedom is duty. The man who said this was a fool. Duty is a negation of freedom. The price of freedom is responsibility, the responsibility to take care of one's self. Duty is the price of being taken care of by another. Duty is the way of the slave.

As I said, the slaves in such a society would choose to be slaves. When faced with the grim spectre of personal accountability and the need for self reliance the mass man, the herd man, will run in terror. Such people need to be taken care of. In return for being cared for these individuals must accept certain duties to those who provide that care. This attitude is the exact opposite of the prevailing attitude today where such programs as welfare and social security are regarded as entitlements, as if one was entitled to being cared for. Those aristocrats willing and able to provide for slaves could, for the price of such care, obtain a ready supply of laborers to serve their purposes.

The care of these slaves need not be too costly. They are, after all, herd creatures. The common rabble is fearful of that which is different. Gather them together in vast ghettos, or suburbs, in mass produced identical housing with mass produced identical furniture and they will be contented. They do not want innovation or originality. They do not want craftsmanship. All they want is what the next guy has got.

By housing the prole masses in such ghettos the aristocracy will serve itself for it will create a generally happy and contented mass. Furthermore, the unrelenting sameness will reinforce herd mentality in them and thereby keep them weak. This same drab uniformity will help to identify those children who show some promise for such children will not be able to live contentedly in such conditions. Upon identifying such promising youngsters the aristocracy could then raise them up from the life of a slave and educate them alongside his own children, perhaps even adopting them. In the same way unworthy children of the aristocracy could be abandoned to the life of a slave. The mass produced housing, clothing, furnishings, TVs and pre-packaged food could be churned out by a small number of slaves freeing up the rest for other tasks.

What's that you say? Aren't TVs a needless luxury? No. Television, if utilized properly, is a very valuable tool. At present television is used largely for the purpose of whipping up the masses into a frenzy of discontent and mindless consumption. Mass media, rather than emphasizing consumer culture, would stress the virtues of submission and the happiness to be found in conformity. In this way television could be used as a tool for indoctrinating prole youth and reinforcing such lessons in adults. It would serve to create in the masses of slaves a sense of "belonging", a feeling that they are a part of something larger than themselves, to teach them that they are not valid individuals in their own right. Granted, television already enforces herd mentality but at present it is a mentality of discontent and noxious egalitarianism.

One of the things which might prove initially difficult is convincing the slaves to abandon the current notion that one should live as long as it is possible for doctors to maintain life. It seems to me that the best way to do this is to concentrate on the young. Teach them that a part of their duty is to live as long as they are useful, and then to go out gracefully. Perhaps "touching" TV movies about dear old grandpa going joyfully to the euthanasia center when he can no longer do his share of the work could help to inculcate such an attitude in the young slaves. If this is done effectively the first generation of slaves need not be sold on the idea. Their children will, out of a sense of duty, take them to the euthanasia centers happily. Household domestics might fare somewhat better than common laborers insofar as lifespan is concerned since they might eventually come to be seen as beloved pets and be cared for in their old age while common workers will be discarded like the broken tools that they are.

In time, the slave class might be largely phased out. I do not mean to suggest that no such herd creatures would be born. The slave "type" will always exist. They will just no longer be needed to fill many of the old slave roles. As technology improves the production of androids would create a cheaper, more efficient alternative to human slaves. Certain very dangerous jobs might still utilize human labor since they will probably be considered far more expendable. What would be done with the surplus slaves created by an android labor force? Nothing in particular. They would have no claim to being cared for since they serve no useful purpose. They would not be systematically exterminated by the state since such a program could be very costly. These people would simply be allowed to suffer the fate of all surplus life which nature has ordained. They would go hungry and starve, die of exposure, murder or suicide or, if they opt to try and survive through criminality they would be dealt with as any other criminal, which in itself might often prove fatal.

The system I am here proposing is both rigid and fluid. These two "castes", the aristocracy and the slaves are separated by a great gulf, and yet each is open ended enough to guarantee a great deal of movement between them. The importance of this open-endedness cannot be stressed too highly. It was the closed nature of past aristocracies that invariably led to their eventual stagnation and death. To eliminate that factor and embrace all those worthy of adoption into the aristocracy, while at the same time rejecting the unworthy, regardless of their pedigree, should effectively nullify that threat, and assure that the "best and brightest" will face no artificial impediments to their progress.

Government

First we must consider what the proper function of government is. It would appear to me that this should be self evident. The purpose of government is to maintain order. Unfortunately all too many people think that the purpose of government is to take care of everybody. The idea that a government is supposed to guarantee the happiness and welfare of all of its citizens is an idea that must be discarded as soon as possible. Rather than taking upon itself the role of an understanding and nurturing mother, government should instead devote itself to maintaining the social order. The social order I have heretofore written of is essentially two tiered, although those tiers are not narrowly defined and considerable stratification will exist within these tiers, or castes. This order is the most basic, most fundamental you will ever find. Aristocracy vs Proles, Masters vs Slaves, those who can stand alone and those who need to be led, guided and controlled in all things. The purpose of this government then is to maintain a state of affairs where the masters are free to enjoy their actions, the slaves are not permitted to overstep their bounds, and criminals are dealt with swiftly.

Because the primary purpose of government is to maintain order this government might be best understood as a literal "police state". The difference between this and other, so-called, police states is that this one will be dedicated to a far more minimalistic law code. The ideal government is a government that interferes in no one's life if they mind their own business. The same can be said of the police, and the police state.

The fundamental element of government is a local assembly of the aristocracy. No elections or other such nonsense will go on. Each aristocrat will have a say in local affairs. Leaders will arise spontaneously without having to conduct drawn out and undignified campaigns for election which seem to me tailor made to weed out anyone who is worthy of a position of authority. In these local assemblies decisions pertaining to the community as a whole will be made. These assemblies will not meddle in the personal affairs of any of the master caste. Matters affecting a greater area than a single community will be decided in progressively larger assemblies, or senates. These senates will consist of representatives sent by smaller senates. Again, large scale electioneering is to be done away with. These representatives shall rise through an innate quality of leadership. The highest senate would be entrusted with the writing of law, and maintaining a sufficient military force to deter the aggressive impulses of ones neighboring states, or, if necessary, destroy them. This army would consist largely of slaves as very few members of the aristocracy would want to subject themselves to the rigid authoritarianism of military service. Only among the ranks of the officers might you find aristocrats. To help justify the expense of maintaining them these soldiers would be used for police service rather than keeping them garrisoned for long periods. The support and maintenance of these troops will be attended to through a levy of goods and or services from aristocrats in the locality that they serve. Regular police are another matter and I'll discuss them later.

At all levels of government the hierarchies which emerge are natural ones and are not the product of parliamentary regulation or something so insignificant as seniority. In this way leadership rather than petty politics is the way to rise.

It has been said that one of the manifestations of decay in a republic is when each faction no longer seeks to promote their own agenda so much as they seek to hinder the agenda of the other faction(s). Factionalism will arise, it is part of the nature of things, but the sort of petty factionalism that leads to this stupid, meaningless contrariness might be avoided if the aristocracy remains strong. A weak aristocracy that accepts borderline people (or worse) as peers, and even worse, allows such people to represent them in the higher senates is begging destruction. It has happened before; many times. A big part of this creeping decadence was the hereditary transfer of aristocratic status. Doing away with hereditary aristocracy in the system here discussed is a measure intended to keep the aristocracy strong.

Certainly most aristocrats will not wish to be part of the government. This is quite understandable. Those with both leadership qualities, and a will to rule will naturally gravitate to such positions though, and as long as they embody the strongly self reliant aristocratic ethic all is well. Such leaders will instinctively reject egalitarian philosophies seeking to elevate born slaves to a higher state than they merit. They will also be self assured enough to lack a desire to dominate their fellow aristocrats and will instead maintain a laissez-faire attitude with regard to them. Only slaves and criminals must be dominated. Dominating slaves will require a minimal effort since they desperately want, in fact they need to be dominated. Dominating criminals is a bit more difficult, but is just as necessary.

One modern role of government that will be dispensed with is the idea that a government should be in the business of managing the economy. Except in cases demonstrating a clear need to take action, such as catastrophic environmental damage resulting from some business endeavor, government should not meddle in economic matters. Such matters will regulate themselves far better without governmental intervention. The nature of this economy might well be much different than any present system. For example, mass production would almost certainly be replaced by a greater emphasis on quality and craftsmanship. Also I suspect that barter will undergo something of a resurgence. None of this however is the concern of the government.

A government such as this could, by doing less, do much more. By involving itself wholly in those affairs which are within its natural purview, and eschewing any involvement in areas outside of its proper place, such a government could be much more effective in accomplishing its valid and worthwhile goals. Through overextension and excessive paternalism government sets itself on a course towards inevitable corruption and destruction. We must learn the valuable lessons of the past so that we might avoid the pitfalls that lie ahead.

Law & Order

There are two basic options when it comes to establishing a nation's laws. The first route is to establish law which tries to cover every possible contingency, and which tries to protect people as much as possible from harm, whether this harm originates in the actions of others or, as is more likely, themselves. The second route is to opt for a more open ended legal minimalism.

It should be clear that the present system is working towards the first approach. In part this is because the masses seek to be protected from every possible unpleasantness that might exist in the world. In addition, the making of laws is all too often entrusted to lawyers. The initial mistake is in believing that, owing to their familiarity with law, lawyers are ideally suited to make laws. This is not the case. Even the best system of laws will be ruined by the time they are finished. The obvious reason for this is that lawyers have a vested interest in establishing a legal system so convoluted, and full of loopholes that they, the lawyers, become indispensable. The place of the lawyer is to serve the law, not to make it. Government by lawyers is bound to take a nation down the road to excessive legalism. A far better way is to strive for legal minimalism.

In the laws applied to the masters the notion that law should be based upon some moral ground would be dispensed with. These laws will be far more practical in nature. Anything which involves only consenting adults is not the proper concern of law. Under such a system such "offenses" as drug use, gambling and prostitution would no longer be regarded as criminal since no one who does not wish to be involved is harmed in any way.

Some might object that those under the influence of drugs might commit other crimes, or that the gambler inflicts suffering upon his family, or that prostitution is degrading. These objections are ridiculous. If a drug user commits crimes then prosecute them for those crimes. If a member of a family is gambling away their livelihood then they should leave that person to suffer alone. If a woman does not wish to prostitute herself then there is nothing requiring her to do so. If she is being forced then prosecute whoever it is who is doing this. Reason would thus replace moralizing. The basic rule in such a system is this—*mind your own business!* As long as you do this you'll not run afoul of the law. Personal disputes will, as often as not, be settled by individuals without the need for the courts.

As in the rest of society there will be a distinction drawn between the masters and the slaves. The same sort of legal minimalism which will be applied to the dealings of the masters will not be applied to the slaves. Slaves will be subject to whatever rules that those who care for them see fit to enforce upon them. If a slave does not wish to be bound by such rules then they can always opt to leave slavery behind and be treated as a master, if they're up to it, that is.

It should not be surmised that I am endorsing drug use, or anything else, simply because I do not think it should be considered a crime. This is the mistake of the moralizer. To the moralizer anything which he cannot "in good conscience" endorse should be forbidden. I personally think that prohibiting such things serves no useful purpose and that the idea that these things should be outlawed so as to protect people who might otherwise become habituated to drugs, or gambling, or whatever else is foolish. It is always a mistake to shelter the fool from the effects of his folly. It would also be a mistake to assume that in wanting to see such things decriminalized that I subscribe to the current idea that such behavior is an addiction, a manifestation of disease, which should be treated rather than punished. I am not impressed with the current trend to treat such habits as addictions and do not feel an abundance of compassion for such creatures. In fact, I do not care about these people at all so long as they mind their own business. I would recommend the works of Dr. Thomas Szasz to anyone who buys all the therapy-speak about the tragedy of addiction. *Ceremonial Chemistry* is particularly good in this regard.

Earlier I mentioned that military units should be used for police duties rather than leaving them idly garrisoned. Military units must be used for something, and unless you wish to embark upon a course of empire building, police duty is probably the most beneficial use for them. Such forces would be rotated between military and police duties. These soldiers would be used as patrol officers while most of the full time police units would be detectives. While soldiers and police patrollers will be slaves many detectives might well be members of the master caste. At the very least they will be among the best and brightest of the slaves. These detectives would be expected to have a ready understanding of all investigative techniques. Specialized forensic investigators would also be devoted to full time police duty. There should be zero tolerance of incompetence in so important a position. Simple mistakes should be grounds for discipline or dismissal from duty. Willful misconduct or shabby work resulting in failure to solve crimes should bring harsher consequences, perhaps even execution.

OF GODS AND GODS

In various writings I produced in the past, I have stated that there is no place for the gods in Satanism. In some cases I was referring to "Satanists" worshiping non-Christian dieties. To my mind, a Satanist worshiping a pre-Christian god, like Thor, is every bit as ridiculous as a Satanist worshiping Jehovah. But there is another way of looking at that statement besides the obvious, literal, interpretation.

A really good Satanic credo is obtained by a simple modification of a statement taken from the Judeo-Christian commandments. That credo is I AM THE LORD MY GOD, AND I WILL HAVE NO OTHER GODS BEFORE ME. There are some who do indeed place "other gods" before themselves.

What do I mean? Well, put simply, a god, in this context is anything that you exalt above yourself. To some, race is their god. To others it is duty, or tradition, or some group identity. Whatever you think of as being more important than your own desires is your god. There is no place in Satanism for such attitudes. Whatever happened to the idea that Satanism was the selfish religion, indeed, *the* religion of the self? Other religions or movements stress selflessness. Only Satanism puts the self, the individual, at the forefront. To the Satanist the individual will is, and must be, preeminent. To deny the self in the interest of some great collective will is the antithesis of Satanism. You might as well be a Christian.

Words like tradition and duty are sometimes bandied about in discussions of Satanism. Think about that. What is the purpose of such talk? To bestow the voice of authority on the things bearing the stamp of duty and tradition. But what is duty, or tradition, if not the great dragon Nietzsche warned about a parable of the lion and the child. The dragon "Thou Shalt". "He who sayeth "thou shalt to me is my mortal foe." Sound familiar? Of course, but many do not consider the fact that the voice that whispers in your ear of the traditions that must be respected, or the duty that must be fulfilled, or the higher purpose, whatever it might be, that must be served, is saying thou shalt to you. And some of you swallow it all without question. You do not hear the words "thou shalt" , and since you do not hear the magic formula of "thou shalt", you don't mind. Well, you need not say "thou shalt" to say thou shalt.

Some will seek to say that the Church of Satan has a tradition, and since we have tradition that the rejection of tradition is hypocritical. Do not be deceived. The Church of Satan has a tradition only in the sense that it rejects tradition. A tradition of anti-traditionalism if you will. QUESTION ALL THINGS—truly that is the creed to live by. It may well be that after questioning their ideas you will agree with some principle, or principles, espoused by the advocates of tradition or duty, or whatever else. But then you will accept it on your terms. It will serve you, rather than you serving it. You will turn the gods of others into your servants. Is this not the true way of the Satanist?

FILM NOIR, TRAGEDY AND THE SATANIST

Over the years, I have heard from several people who find the repeated references to the genre of film noir in various Church of Satan writings to be inexplicable. What, they wonder, does all this have to do with Satanism? The answer to this is not a simple one. In *The Secret Life of a Satanist,* Dr. LaVey addresses this issue, and normally I have referred these various inquirers to this book. Aside from such elements as aesthetics, cynicism, irony, atmospherics, which provide ample reason to watch, there is another element of film noir that makes it the ideal choice for Satanic Viewers. Film noir is practically the only modern form of tragic drama.

Tragedy is not in favor today. This situation is not surprising as the masses are far too weak to enjoy tragedy. As Nietzsche observed in *The Birth of Tragedy,* only strong individuals can truly enjoy tragedy. The weak find it far too depressing. Do you doubt this? Just look at some of the things popular amongst the herd, if you can stomach it. What will you find? Happy endings. Mindlessly cheerful pap. There is an odd genre popular amongst the herd. Some have characterized it as tragic, but it is not. This type of movies or plays depict those suffering from disease, or victimized by others in some way. The aim of such things is quite different from the tragic view. These betray their puritanical origins with their tiresome moralizing and "uplifting" messages. They pose as educational tools trying to eliminate the various ills depicted. The tragic view is not that the ills of the world must be purged but rather, that the ills of the world must be endured.

The Nietzschean superman is characterized by an ability to look on even the less enjoyable aspects of life unflinchingly. This too describes the Satanist. Unlike the herd, we need no sugar coated pseudo-reality or uplifting messages. We grow stronger through the realization of this fact. This fact is reinforced through tragic drama, including film noir. Of course, the recognition of the true nature of life should not render you grim and humorless. Quite to the contrary, we should learn to seize the day and writing from it all the happiness and pleasure it can yield. To laugh, even in the face of adversity, is the prerogative of the strong.

Some, notably Ayn Rand, have written disparagingly of tragedy. They characterize the tragic worldview as one postulating a malevolent universe. This is a mistaken notion. The tragic view, while not necessarily atheistic, rejects the notion that there is somebody out there that cares about us. It states that even if there were gods, we'd still be on our own. The universe is not malevolent, it is uncaring. Were we to see the universe as being malevolent, as something which sought our downfall, we would be mere pessimists. We are not pessimists. The Satanist is a pragmatist. We know that life has ups and downs. We savor the upside, we endure the downside, knowing, as Nietzsche said, what doesn't kill us strengthens us. As the tragic heroes of the past, we will never surrender. We will not allow ourselves to give up and die.

It is important to stress the distinction between the pessimists, and those who share the tragic view of life. The pessimist says, "Everything comes to naught in the end, so why bother? Nothing matters." Such nihilistic outlook is self-defeating. Those who think this way set them selves up for failure. Those who share in a tragic sense know that no matter how well you plan for things, things can go wrong. As Doc Riedenschneider asks in *The Asphalt Jungle*, "Blind accidents! What can you do against blind accidents?" The answer is, of course, nothing. This doesn't mean that you should accept failure or defeat as inevitable, merely possible. Defeatist attitudes are alien to us. We struggle, even in the face of defeat, because it is better to die on your feet than on your knees. No other option is available to us. The tragic hero, or anti-hero, is a quintessentially Satanic character. He always struggles back to his feet, or dies in the struggle. He accepts the cards that fate deals to him and makes the best of them. Even if he despairs he doesn't give up. If for nothing else, this tragic aspect is ample reason for the Satanist to watch films noir.

THE SATANIST IN THE GARDEN

To many, Greek philosophy begins and ends with the "holy" trinity of Socrates, Plato, and Aristotle. In fact that there were many other philosophers who often had views quite different from these three. Some find the roots of Satanism in these philosophers, but I feel a much greater affinity with a philosopher carrying on the work of one of the pre-Socratic philosophers-a philosophy quite different from that espoused by that well known trinity.

The pre-Socratic philosophers regarded themselves as physicists as well as philosophers. These men often approached things from two sides. On one hand, they looked at the nature of the world, the primal substance of existence. On the other, they examined ethical and sociological matters. One example is Heraclitus. On the physical side, he believed that life was characterized by struggle, and that the best men eschew the way of the mob. Another of these pre-Socratic philosophers was Democritus, who founded the school of philosophy known as Atomism.

Democritus' Atomism held that there were only two things in the world: atoms and void. Atoms are invisible things from which all matter is made, which move through void in straight, pre-determined courses. One of Democritus' successors, Epicurus, deviated from this, saying that these atoms did not move in straight, pre-determined courses. He suggested that there was a slight swerve in the movement of the atoms. This slight swerve added an element of unpredictability to the world so, in a sense, Epicurus that is of principal interest to us here. Instead, I will concentrate on this ethical and social ideas.

Unfortunately, most of the Epicurus' writings are lost to us. I suspect that the Christian Mob took great delight in consigning his work to the flames. One of the early Christian leaders, Jerome, denounced one of the foremost Epicureans in Rome, the poet Lucretius, as a madman. What does survive is of great value. It is, in my opinion of infinitely more value than the writings of the Stoics and Platonists.

Epicurus taught in his garden in Athens. Unlike most other philosophers, Epicurus also taught women. Philosophically, Epicurus taught that the highest value was pleasure. This was something unheard of at the time. Many had accepted the idea that Man did, in fact act in the pursuit of pleasure, but this was seen as a defect in Man's nature. Epicurus said that man should regard pleasure as his goal. This philosophy is often interpreted as mere unlimited license, but it is not. Epicurus was quite clear in stating that mere licentiousness often brought with it far more pain than pleasure. Epicureanism can not be easily pigeonholed as a sort of "Eat, drink and be merry for tomorrow we die" type of philosophy, although this is the common perception. As Satanists, we should know from firsthand experience that the common perception is often quite different than the reality. "No pleasure is a bad thing in itself: but the means which produce some pleasures bring with them disturbances many times greater than the pleasures." Do these sound like the words of a mere libertine?

Epicurus was also a dedicated proponent of common sense. While other philosophers believed that the world that we can see, and hear, and touch, is somehow unreal—or less real than some kind of "ideal" world. Epicurus believed that only a fool rejected the evidence of his senses. To Epicurus, the phenomenal world was not just an apparent world, but the one and only world. This categorical rejection of other-worldliness is all too scarce in the shadowy world of philosophical metaphysics, and I for one find it quite refreshing. In keeping with this distinctly materialistic philosophy, Epicurus rejected any notion of life after death. To Epicurus, the idea that you might feel pain after you died was ridiculous. The dualistic notion that there is a spiritual realm that exists separate and apart from the physical world was alien to his philosophy. Pain and suffering are products of flesh, therefore, when that flesh lies in cold and dead, there can be no pain.

All things considered, Epicurus is a philosopher whom Satanists would do well to explore. I do not generally recommend philosophers. Most are fools engaging in debates every bit as meaningless as the old theological dispute over how many angels could dance on the head of a pin. When a philosopher deals with reality, it is a sufficiently rare occurrence to be worth looking into.

DUELING DUALITIES

For centuries, Western society has been dominated by a philosophical system that can be best described as antagonistic dualism, the belief that the world is compromised of pairs of irreconcilable opposites. Under this system, life is reduced to a series of either/or choices. This worldview is so pervasive that it provides the basis of most of the philosophies which provide the foundations of modern life I will not be attempting a comprehensive look at it in this article. Instead I will touch upon a few examples of the results of such ideas, and touch upon the origins of this insidious philosophy.

The roots of antagonistic dualism go back some 2500-3000 years to ancient Persia. It was there that the Zoroastrians developed what was probably the first religion/ethical system based upon the idea of a metaphysical struggle between good and evil. Today, thanks to the Zoroastrians, people tend to think of good and evil as fixed absolutes, causes rather than effects, but this was not always the case. Many ancient societies thought of this dichotomy quite differently. Generally, good was whatever was beneficial to you, your family or your tribe/nation. Evil on the other hand was simply whatever was harmful to these same groups. Good and evil were seen as effects and not causes. Antagonistic duality lies behind this inversion of ideas. Consider the Greco-Roman, or Germano-Celtic mythologies. You'll find no such notions of ethical dualism as you find in Zoroastrian or Judaic mythology, you simply cannot compare a figure such as Zeus, or Odin to an Ahura-Mazda or Yahveh. Contrary to the conventional opinion however, the leap from Zeuses and Odins to Yahveh and his ilk is hardly an advancement, it is instead a great leap backwards. The ancients all recognized the duality of nature but they did not attach any moral values to such things, they were simply recognized as counterparts in the overall scheme of things. Antagonistic duality, as manifested first among the Persians and later among the Jews, was bad enough but it was primarily concerned with good and evil. After the idea spread to the decadent philosophers of the late Hellenic periods, such as Plato and Socrates, it broadened it's scope to include almost all of the world in its pointless divisiveness.

Today, these dichotomies can be generally divided into two categories. The internal dichotomies are the first group and would include such things as good vs. evil, intellect vs. instinct and reason vs. passion. The second group, the external dichotomies would include such things as civilization vs. nature, life vs. death and male vs. female. It is with these dichotomies that I will be concerning myself hereafter.

The idea of good vs. evil has a long history in the world, and is central to the Judeo-Christian ethic which has so polluted the world. The ideas of this group I have already dealt with, so I'll not repeat all of that. The other internal dichotomies are very similar to the good vs. evil dichotomy in many respects. Each characterized by a refusal to recognize the totality of man's inner makeup. And each of these groups of people are prone to the same adverse effects which derive from this self-imposed internal conflict.

One of the most common internal dichotomies today is intellect vs. instinct. There are some who believe that the only knowledge of any value is intellectual in nature, learned knowledge. These people do not believe that inborn, instinctive understanding is of any value, in fact there are some who deny that man has any instincts. To be sure, man's instincts are not so absolute as the instincts of insects or birds but it would be a mistake to claim that man is devoid of instinct. As a primate, man has a fairly open-ended set of instincts, which leaves a great deal to be learned. There are however deeply felt drives which are inborn. There would be no conflict between instinct and intellect were it not for man's tendency to build up unnatural institutions to make the world more agreeable to his overdelicate sensibilities. When an instinctive drive runs counter to the rules man has established, a new action is taught to replace the instinctive act in the individual's mind. To claim that all intellect is without value is prevalent, but equally erroneous. These people follow the Rousseauesque doctrine of the noble savage. The error of these people lies in the fact that the human animal does not come with a complete program as does a bee, or ant. A human being must acquire a certain degree of intellectual learning in order to survive. Anti-intellectualism may be rooted in a reasonable distrust of inordinate intellectualism, but it goes too far in the other direction. Just as the ultimate end of the intellectualists is a world where everyone does precisely as he has been taught to do, a world where every move is analyzed and spontaneity is a thing of the past, the end of the anti-intellectualists is a world of ignorance, and mistrust of any learning.

A very closely related conflict is reason vs. passion. The worshippers of reason regard reason as the be-all and end-all of human existence. There people fail to recognize that reason is only a tool. This over dependence on reason goes back to Greece, notably the philosopher Aristotle. The ideal of such people is being that is totally dominated by reason. A being that is not swayed by passion. These people are continually stressing that a man is not "just an animal". Their passions remind them of their animal nature and must therefore be done away with. As I see it, their ideal is a bloodless machine. Ultimately, by their very nature these deifiers of reason will fall into the same trap as the overly intellectual. Once again the other side is equally mistaken. Traditionally, artists fall within the category of those who stress the passions over reason. The virulently anti-rational are a minority in this group. Those who reject reason, and are totally ruled by passions are not taking advantage of some of the unique characteristics of the human animal. These slaves to their passions will often drift aimlessly through life. They will follow their feelings even if they lead to their own destruction.

All of these groups are united in their desire to tear themselves into two parts. Whether that division is between good/evil, reason/passion, or instinct/intellect is ultimately irrelevant. They can all be roughly divided into two types, exterminators and suppressors. Those I call exterminators are driven to purge themselves of every trace of whatever undesirable element they can find in their nature. The other group, the suppressors, are less driven. They usually understand that they will never purge themselves entirely of the offensive elements and so they are satisfied in suppressing it as much as possible. These types often believe that in time these offensive traits, if suppressed, will atrophy and die. While both groups are fighting futile battles against themselves, battles which they are doomed to lose, the suppressors can usually come through with fewer of the more unpleasant side-effects.

The worst that will befall a suppressor is, more often than not, a few neuroses of varying degree. It is another story with the exterminators. With each failure to destroy the hated element of their nature they will grow more single-mined and fanatical. It is from the ranks of the exterminators that all of the inquisitors, puritians and witch-hunters have come. While the suppressor will avoid the middle ground of balance, the exterminator will find it so repellent that he will go to any extreme, even the opposite extreme to avoid it. This is reflected in the well known fact that the quickest to convert to any extremist philosophy are those who, until recently, adhered to the opposing doctrine. Until the exterminator breaks away from his position, which is usually a very sudden decision, they will almost certainly be unwilling to consider any other opinion. It is a fools errand to try to reason with an exterminator, even those who have exalted reason.

The external dichotomies cannot be divided into exterminators and suppressors because they operate in a very different way. These are not struggles of man vs. himself. The external dichotomies are a manifestation of man's struggle against the world around him. The struggles are the same as the internalized ones in this regard, thought they are equally pointless. A good example of the kind of idiotic conflict that falls under the heading is civilization vs. nature. The forces of civilization are responsible for the continuing deforestation of the Earth, the extermination of the wild animal species to make room for surplus humans and other domesticated animals, and a general preference for the artificial to the natural. On the other side are more of Rousseau's disciples. These people would delight in restoring an age of innocence which they believe existed in the long ago dim past. They yearn for return to the garden of Eden, but would only accomplish a return to the cave. While no one can argue that all of the so-called advances, it should be obvious that it is not in our interest to throw it all away in pursuit of a golden age that never did, and never will, exist. Another of the external dichotomies is life vs. death. Today there is a widely held belief that there is an innate sanctity in human life, and that life, at any level, is better than death. As a direct result of this idea, the human population of the Earth is escalating at an ever increasing rate. As a natural consequence of this overcrowding, famine and pestilence occasionally break out and natural disasters such as earthquakes, hurricanes, and flooding wreak greater havoc. Such things, while they are vital elements of nature's population control system, are violations of man's rules. Whenever nature intervenes with famine or some such measure, in comes a flood of "humanitarian" aid—food, clothing, and medicine—in an effort to thwart nature's design. If mankind does not change its course, nature will change him. You cannot circumvent nature indefinitely. Like it or not, man will have to start playing by nature's rules. On a more personal level, it is not unusual to see people who will cling to life, even a bedridden life dependent upon machines, rather than accept death and go out with a little dignity. What sane person can say that it is better to live as a frail, senile shadow of their former selves than to die when they have reached the logical conclusion of their lives?

Another product of this worldview is the "battle of the sexes." It has promoted a uselessly divisive outlook which has done nothing except create unwarranted hostility and pointless bickering. Each side argues over which sex is superior. You might as well argue over whether a saw is a better tool than hammer. It is certainly true that nowhere in nature is equality to be found, but inequality does not follow gender lines. We are individuals and must be judged as such. A division of the human race into two uniform gender blocs is ridiculous. It is true that some women are utterly worthless for anything other than childbearing, but there are some that are superior to many men I've known who are useful only for mindless menial labor. No, ultimately gender is not a valid factor in establishing the social hierarchy. Even more insane that the extremists on behalf of either side are what passes for moderate in this issue. These people would destroy the enmity between male and female through an attempt at destroying the differences. They seek to establish an androgynous, unisex world where the innate difference between the sexes are suppresses through socialization and "test-tube" reproduction. The solution to the problems brought about though antagonistic dualism is not to be found in the or suit of a thoroughly unnatural state of affairs, it lies in an understanding of the fact that despite their innate differences, the sexes are not bound into an adversary relationship; an understanding that it is possible to view them as complimentary halves of a larger whole.

Ultimately, though the mind perceives the duality inherent in nature, it seeks to restore a unified whole. Antagonistic dualism, in all its varied forms, believes that only one side of the duality is natural. They believe that the rest is sort of cancerous growth which must be exercised. Their ultimate goal is a world torn in half, a barren monotonous life free of the inner conflict that they themselves have promoted. It is time for a restoration of that older, healthier view that there is a natural balance in nature between the duality's halves, a recognition that all are necessary in their place. A good illustration of this is found in the symbology of the sigil of Baphomet. As Dr. LaVey has stated in *The Satanic Bible*, the horn of the goat symbolize duality. Each horn is separated and distinct from the other, yet both are but part of the goat. Since the goat is a symbol of carnality, and thus of nature, it is therefore seen that everything is part of nature an that to exalt some part of nature above the whole s foolish. It should be obvious to everyone that only by recognizing the totality of nature, including human nature—despite what superficially appear to be contradictions, can life continue in any worthwhile sense. The road which western culture is presently traveling leads only to destruction. Until mankind no longer feels compelled to engage in counterproductive struggles with himself and nature there can be no real progress. This Persian monster, and its offspring, must be destroyed. If we do not destroy them they will certainly destroy us.

IT'S NOT A BADGE OF HONOR

Satan represents man as just another animal, sometimes better, more often worse than those that walk on all-fours, who, because of his "divine spiritual and intellectual development," has become the most vicious animal of all!

—Anton Szandor LaVey

No doubt all of you recognize the quote above as the seventh Satanic Statement by Anton LaVey. Sadly I have often come across Satanists, or those who call themselves Satanists, who somehow interpret the viciousness that Doktor LaVey mentioned as a good thing?

All too often I've come across dullards who see it as a call to viciousness. Their muddled thinking runs like this: "Anton LaVey said that man is the most vicious animal of all so I should be as vicious as I can be." Once I would give some of these, the ones who seemed to have a handle on just about everything else, the benefit of the doubt, and explain the error of their interpretation. As time went on I have almost always come to regret all attempts to explain such things and now I usually just assume that those who don't get it, won't get it and leave them to stumble about in their benighted ignorance until such time as they can prove me wrong. Such empty-headedness as misunderstanding this pretty straightforward statement is something that pretty clearly demonstrates to me that you are not worth my time.

What is it that these people have a problem understanding? Do they honestly believe that Anton LaVey would have used the term "divine spiritual and intellectual development" with anything other than derision? Do they really think viciousness is something positive? The term vicious pretty uniformly describes the behavior of a broken animal. What is the proverbial "mad dog" that should be destroyed if not a classic example of viciousness?

How is it that such people fail to grasp the obvious? Man is indeed just another animal, but because he has deluded himself to believe that God has given him a soul that sets him above mere animals, or that his intellectual development has allowed him to transcend animality, he has lost touch with his true nature. In trying desperately to be what he foolishly believes himself to be, a non-animal, he simply becomes a broken animal that is driven to aberrant, and vicious behavior. This viciousness escalates to ever greater levels the further divorced from the "merely animal" he believes himself to be.

W.W.A.D.

A few years ago empty headed members of the Jesus Youth began sporting jewelry and T-shirts emblazoned with W.W.J. D. An acronym for that burning question "What would Jesus do?" Today it seems that we have a crop of idiots who feel as if they know just what Anton LaVey would do if he were still alive, and it is not what the Church of Satan is currently doing. Not surprisingly, these lackwits invariably feel as if the Doktor would have done exactly as they would do instead. It should therefore come as no surprise that those who are in such "obvious synch" with the thoughts and intentions of Anton LaVey also feel entirely justified in referring to him as Anton. *"Anton wouldn't do that!"* they whine whenever the Church of Satan implements a policy that they find not to their liking. This sort of thing always brings to mind Florence King's maxim regarding the rabble's incessant need for such a false sense of intimacy with their idols, "Familiarity IS contempt".

The current leaders of the Church of Satan worked with Anton LaVey for many years. Many other members of the church hierarchy knew the man. I have had many conversations with these people over the years and not once have I heard any of them spouting such drivel. They follow the same guiding principals that the Doktor followed and arrive at their decisions in the same way, by weighing all of the available information and applying their own judgement.

The fact of the matter is that none of us really know exactly what Doktor LaVey would have done in any given situation. We do know that he did not create a monolithic and unchanging organization. As policies became outmoded they were altered or phased out, but the core philosophy remained intact. The same can be said of any vital organization. An organization that does not move with the times will not survive.

So much silliness has been set forth about the current High Priest of the Church of Satan. While no one can say that what

Peter Gilmore has done is exactly what Anton LaVey would have done, I can say that Peter Gilmore is a man whose mastery of Satanic principles is impeccable and I trust his judgement. As someone who has been around for many years I am always somewhat amused at the charges that the Chuch of Satan changed direction after Anton LaVey died. What I see is not a drastic change but rather a few minor course corrections such as have been occurring as needed since 1966. If you do not like Peter Gilmore, that is certainly your prerogative, but don't delude yourself into thinking that Anton LaVey would have done things differently, and you know exactly how he would have done them.

You don't, and insisting that you do only makes you looks foolish.

The funniest part of this pathetic trend is that before Doktor LaVey's death these same people now denounced for allegedly deviating from the path Anton LaVey would have followed were often excoriated for being mere lackeys slavishly following in Anton LaVey's footsteps. Then, as now, such gibberings from the rabble are unimportant. We have better things to do that to try to please delusional, self-important fools. Let them mutter amongst themselves in their chat-room cabals and Myspace covens. Let them gnash their teeth and shake their fists at us in their ineffectual rage. They will not deter us from our myriad indulgences, and that is the most Satanic act of all.

THE MASS OF SAINT FRANCIS

The inspiration behind this ceremony is the most famous of the old "Hellfire Clubs", that established by Francis Dashwood. Once upon a time it was commonly believed that the members of the Hellfire Club actually worshipped Satan, although more recent authors have rejected the notion. While some writers have bent over backwards to whitewash them and scrub away any hints of blasphemy, I think this goes too far in the other direction. While they do not seem to have been devil worshippers, there was certainly a palpable air of brimstone about them.

Much has been written about this group, almost all of it being speculation as the actual records of the meetings were destroyed long ago, but based on what is known it is safe to say that the club was dedicated to two things above all, mocking false pieties, and indulgence. From the sparse surviving accounts of those involved we know that prostitutes were hired for the meetings and at least sometimes were dressed as nuns. There was much eating, drinking and making merry. The members apparently took great pleasure in boasting of their "wicked ways," (it is in that spirit that the confessional portion of the ritual is conducted).

I wanted to write a ceremony in the spirit of the Hellfire Club, which, as an organization dedicated to indulgence and the skewering of sacred cows, I view as quite Satanic. As a nod to the tales of black masses conducted by the club I based the framework on a traditional black mass, but skewed the focus more to the side of indulgence. The ceremony should act as a prelude to a party. The precise nature of this party is left to each particular group performing the rite, but it is meant to serve as a celebration of indulgence.

Remember always the motto of the Hellfire Club:

Do as you will!

PRELIMINARY

Ideally this ceremony will be performed in a subterranean chamber.

Roles in ritual:

- *Celebrant*
- *Three Nuns*
- *Supplicant*
- *Congregation/Confessee*

Requirements for the ceremony:

- *Altar.*
- *Sigil of Baphomet.*
- *Bell.*
- *Phallus.*
- *Censer* with *Incense.*
- *Chalice* filled with your choice of elixir, (In keeping with the Hellfire Club's fondness for it I recommend that it be filled with Port, but this is not essential).
- *Sweets* on a *Tray.* These can be either small chocolates or cakes, one for each participant. They should be sufficiently small to eat whole in one bite.
- *Bishop's Mitre* adorned with a winged phallus in the form of an inverted cross.
- Three *Nun's Habits.*
- *Ritual Book* containing the Ceremony.
- Paper for writing *Requests.*

I. POLLUTIONARY

THE CEREMONY BEGINS WITH THE RINGING OF THE *BELL* NINE TIMES.

II. INVOCAZIONE

THE CELEBRANT ENTERS WEARING THE *BISHOP'S MITRE* ATTENDED BY THREE WOMEN IN *NUN'S HABITS*. ONE CARRIES A *PHALLUS*, ANOTHER CARRIES A *CHALICE*, AND THE THIRD CARRIES THE *RITUAL BOOK*.

UPON ARRIVING AT THE *ALTAR* THE NUN BEARING THE *RITUAL BOOK* HANDS IT TO THE CELEBRANT AND REMOVES HER *HABIT*. ONCE NUDE, SHE TAKES HER PLACE SITTING UPRIGHT UPON THE *ALTAR*. CELEBRANT RETURNS THE *BOOK* TO HER TO HOLD IT OPEN IN HER LAP. THE OTHER TWO NUNS WILL STAND ON EITHER SIDE OF THE ALTAR, HOLDING THEIR RITUAL ITEMS.

THE CELEBRANT NOW TURNS TO THE CONGREGATION AND SAYS:

CELEBRANT: In Nomine dei Nostri Satanas Luciferi Excelsi.

THE CELEBRANT TAKES THE *PHALLUS* FROM THE ATTENDANT AND CIRCUMAMBULATES THE CHAMBER BLESSING THE ASSEMBLY IN THE NAME OF THE APPROPRIATE CROWN PRINCE OF HELL AT EACH POINT. ON COMPLETION HE HOLDS THE *PHALLUS* UPRIGHT BEFORE HIM.

Peni Tento non Penitenti.

THE CELEBRANT NOW READS THE SECOND ENOCHIAN KEY, THEN ADDS *INCENSE* TO THE *CENSER* SAYING:

We make this offering to you, Satan, Lord of the World. Accept it and smile upon us.

THE CELEBRANT TAKES THE *CENSER* AND CIRCUMAMBULATES THE CHAMBER WITH IT. ONCE HE RETURNS TO FACE THE *ALTAR*.

CELEBRANT: Before the Mighty and ineffable Prince of Darkness, and in the presence of all the demons of the Pit, and this assembled company I proclaim that Satan rules the Earth, and we recognize and honor Him in all things, desiring in return His manifold assistance in the successful completion of all our endeavors and the fulfillment of our desires.

III. AFFERMAZIONE

THE CELEBRANT TURNS TO THE CONGREGATION.

CELEBRANT: I call upon you all to affirm this.

CONGREGATION (*responds*): Satan rules the Earth!

CELEBRANT: Indulgence instead of abstinence!

CONGREG. (*responds*): HAIL SATAN!

CELEBRANT: Vital existence instead of spiritual pipe dreams!

CONGREG. (*responds*): HAIL SATAN!

CELEBRANT: Undefiled wisdom instead of hypocritical self-deceit!

CONGREG. (*responds*): HAIL SATAN!

CELEBRANT: Kindness to those who deserve it instead of love wasted on ingrates!

CONGREG. (*responds*): HAIL SATAN!

CELEBRANT: Vengeance instead of turning the other cheek!

CONGREG. (*responds*): HAIL SATAN!

CELEBRANT: Responsibility to the responsible!

CONGREG. (*responds*): HAIL SATAN!

CELEBRANT: Man is but a Beast!

CONGREG. (*responds*): HAIL SATAN!

IV. INDULGENZA

THE CELEBRANT TAKES ONE OF THE *SWEETS* FROM THE *TRAY* AND ELEVATES IT BEFORE THE *SIGIL OF BAPHOMET.* HE TURNS TO THE CONGREGATION.

CELEBRANT: This represents to us sweet indulgence. Take this in the name of the only holy spirit... the spirit of indulgence.

THE CELEBRANT TAKES THE *TRAY* AND GIVES ONE *SWEET* TO EACH PERSON THERE SAYING:

Strength through Joy.

WHEN ALL HAVE TAKEN ONE *SWEET* HE WILL ELEVATE THE *CHALICE.*

Behold the Chalice of Voluptuous Flesh. In the name of Satan drink this in the spirit of indulgence.

THE CELEBRANT GIVES THE *CHALICE* TO EACH PERSON SAYING:

The flesh reigns supreme.

WHEN ALL HAVE TAKEN A DRINK FROM THE *CHALICE* HE WILL SAY:

There is no Heaven of glory bright, no Hell where sinners roast. Here and now is our day of torment! Here and now is our day of joy! Here and now is our opportunity! Choose ye this day, this hour, for no redeemer liveth!

THE CELEBRANT NOW ASKS FOR A SUPPLICANT TO OFFER A PRAYER.

SUPPLICANT: Our Brother, who art in Hell, hallowed be Thy name. Thy kingdom is come, Thy will is done, on earth as it is in Hell. We take this night our rightful due, and trespass not on paths of pain. Lead us into temptation, and deliver us from false piety, for Thine is the kingdom, and the power and the glory... Forever!

V. CONFESSIONALE

The celebrant now calls the congregation to "confessional".
Each will come forward and boast of some "sin" they have
enjoyed indulging in. They begin their "confession" by saying:

confessee: Blessed am I for I have sinned... *[details "sin"]*

After detailing the "sin" the celebrant will say to them:

celebrant: Truly you are blessed. Go and sin some more.

Repeat in turn until all willing confessees are done.

Renouncing the spiritual paradise of the weak and lowly, we place our trust in Thee, the God of the flesh, looking to the satisfaction of all our desires, and seeking fulfillment in the land of the living. If any here have desires yet unfulfilled, come forth and state them before the throne of Satan.

Anyone willing will now come forward
and either state or present a written *Request*
to burn in the Black Flame.

So it shall be! Remember always the motto of this order... DO AS YOU WILL!

Celebrant turns to the *Altar*.

O thou mighty light and burning flame of comfort, that unveils the Glory of Satan to the center of the earth; in whom the great secrets of truth have their abiding; that is called in thy kingdom "Strength through joy" and is not to be measured. Be thou a window of comfort unto me. Move therefore, and appear! Open the mysteries of your creation! Be friendly unto me for I am the same! The true worshiper of the highest and ineffable King of Hell!

VI. POLLUTIONARY

THE CEREMONY ENDS WITH THE RINGING OF THE *BELL* NINE TIMES.

CELEBRANT: So it is done!
Let the Revels begin!

CREDO FOR THE MODERN MAN

Sticks and stones may break my bones but words will be very hurtful to my psyche and will cause extensive psychic scarring and immeasurable damage to my sense of self esteem.

The loss of self esteem brought about through this exposure to hate speech will be damaging not only to me, but to my children, and their children for generations to come.

The pain of this can be ameliorated only through long term therapy with a concerned and loving therapist. This therapy should, of course, be provided for me at public expense since requiring me to pay for it myself will only compound the damage.

To learn more about Satanism go to

WWW.CHURCHOFSATAN.COM

Other titles you may enjoy from

UNDERWORLD AMUSEMENTS

WWW.UNDERWORLDAMUSEMENTS.COM

The Sorceries and Scandals of Satan
by Henry M. Tichenor
foreword by R. Merciless
6x9, 176 pages, $15.95
ISBN: 978-0983031406

A Bible Not Borrowed from the Neighbors.
Essays and Aphorisms on Egoism
Edited by Kevin I. Slaughter
6x9, 164 pages, $14.95
ISBN: 978-0988553613

Men versus the Man
Socialism versus Individualism
by H.L. Mencken and Robert Rives La Monte
Preface by John Derbyshire
6x9, 204 pages, $15.95
ISBN: 978-0983031420

The Philosophical Writings of Edgar Saltus
Containing the books "The Philosophy of Disenchantment" and "The Anatomy of Negation"
Foreword by Chip Smith
6x9, 366 pages, $18.95

ANATHEMA!
Litanies of Negation
by Benjamin DeCasseres
Foreword by Eugene O'Neill
Afterword by Kevin I. Slaughter
6x9, 66 pages, $9.99
ISBN: 978-0988553620

Homo, 99 and 44/100% Nonsapeins
Revised with a new Introduction
by Gerald B. Lorentz
6x9, 424 pages, $18.95
ISBN: 978-0988553637

Printed in Great Britain
by Amazon

50555186R00099